FREEDOM IN THE SPIRIT

FREEDOM
IN THE
SPIRIT

AN IGNATIAN RETREAT
WITH SAINT PAUL

BRENDAN BYRNE, SJ

Paulist Press
New York / Mahwah, NJ

Cover photo by kostins/Thinkstock.com (by Getty Images)
Cover design by Phyllis Campos
Book design by Lynn Else

Library of Congress Cataloging-in-Publication Data
Names: Byrne, Brendan (Brendan J.), author.
Title: Freedom in the spirit : an Ignatian retreat with Saint Paul / Brendan Byrne, SJ.
Description: New York : Paulist Press, 2016. | Includes bibliographical references and index.
Identifiers: LCCN 2016007058 (print) | LCCN 2016023595 (ebook) | ISBN 9780809149940 (pbk. : alk. paper) | ISBN 9781587686214 (Ebook)
Subjects: LCSH: Ignatius, of Loyola, Saint, 1491-1556. Exercitia spiritualia. Bible. Epistles of Paul—Criticism, interpretation, etc. | Spiritual life—Catholic Church.
Classification: LCC BX2179.L8 B97 2016 (print) | LCC BX2179.L8 (ebook) | DDC 269/.6—dc23
LC record available at https://lccn.loc.gov/2016007058

ISBN 978-0-8091-4994-0 (paperback)
ISBN 978-1-58768-621-4 (e-book)

Published by Paulist Press
997 Macarthur Boulevard
Mahwah, New Jersey 07430

www.paulistpress.com

Printed and bound in the
United States of America

CONTENTS

CONTENTS

PREFACE

This book brings together two central aspects of my life. I am a Jesuit priest, formed in the Ignatian spiritual tradition, and for over thirty years, my primary ministry has been teaching and researching the New Testament, with a particular focus on St. Paul. A recent request to preach an eight-day retreat to Jesuits, other religious, and lay companions in ministry brought these two aspects together. Based mostly on the retreat conferences, this book aims to make the retreat experience available to a wider audience. I am grateful to Fr. Christopher Gleeson, SJ, Mission Formation Delegate of the Australian Jesuit Province, for his invitation to give a retreat based upon St. Paul and his subsequent warm encouragement to make the retreat conferences more widely available in this way.

While the content of the book falls into the pattern of a retreat, with two reflections for each of the eight days (sixteen in all, plus an introductory reflection), there is no need to restrict its use to the time of retreat. My hope is that, outside the retreat experience, the presentations might provide a helpful guide to Pauline theology based on the

Ignatian spiritual tradition. In this sense, the book may serve as an exposition of the spirituality of St. Paul.

At first sight, those familiar with the *Spiritual Exercises* of St. Ignatius of Loyola might wonder whether Paul and Ignatius can, in fact, be brought together in the context of a retreat. After the "First Week" of the *Exercises*, the remaining three "weeks" consist largely of contemplations on the mysteries of the life of Christ as told in the Gospels, culminating in an intense experience of the Paschal Mystery—the passion and resurrection of Jesus. By contrast, Paul and his letters barely rate a mention in the text of the *Spiritual Exercises*, although they certainly feature in the wider range of Scripture that contemporary directors propose to retreatants for prayerful consideration. Basing a retreat almost exclusively on St. Paul offers an alternative version of the experience—albeit, one firmly in the Ignatian tradition. Consequently, those approaching the *Spiritual Exercises* for the first time might do better to seek a more mainstream presentation. Those who have made Ignatian retreats on several occasions may find here a stimulating alternative.

While contemplation on scenes from the Gospels forms a large element of the *Spiritual Exercises*, reference to pre-passion episodes of Jesus' life and ministry are entirely absent in the writings of Paul, and citations of his teaching few. Paul does, of course, take the humanity of Jesus very seriously, but the focus falls almost exclusively on his death, resurrection, and continued existence as "life-giving Spirit" (1 Cor 15:45) in the believing community. At the center of Paul's grasp of the scheme of salvation stands a profound conviction of Christ's love displayed in his self-sacrificial death on behalf of "all," a love behind which stands the love of the Father, made palpable in the community through the experience of the Spirit. A great number of Pauline texts dance around this triune experience of God, approaching it and drawing conclusions from it in a remarkably rich way. These texts are presented here in the hope that Paul's sense of God's love and the mission that flows from it will amount to a transformative experience of divine grace. Readers familiar with the *Spiritual Exercises* may well find here some hint of the pattern of an Ignatian retreat along more traditional lines. The Pauline texts, however, have not been forced into a Procrustean bed to achieve such an effect.

Nor has it been possible, of course, to include and comment on the full range of material attributed to Paul in the New Testament. Readers familiar with his writings and indeed Pauline scholars may wonder at the omission of some texts and the inclusion of others. Much careful reflection has been given to what passages to include and where to locate them in the course of a retreat that makes some claim to be Ignatian. If material from Romans does feature with notable frequency, that simply reflects my own preoccupation with his greatest letter in the course of a now long scholarly career.

One aspect of Paul that makes his writings supremely suitable for retreat reflection is his profound sense of "vocation": his own vocation as an apostle and that of each and every believer "called" to belong to the end-time people of God. This feature of his theology has been most happily retrieved for the Catholic tradition in the Second Vatican Council's insistence on "the universal call to holiness" (Dogmatic Constitution "On the Church" [*Lumen Gentium*] 39–42). The conviction that each and every believer has been "called" into a communion of life by a God who has loved them from all eternity is pervasive in Paul's letters and notably present in the "Address" with which each begins. Whatever the particular shape of a retreatant's vocation within the church—whether layperson, cleric, or religious—several days of sustained prayer and reflection on the writings of Paul will surely enrich that vocation profoundly.

All the writers in the New Testament presumed and drew richly on the Scriptures of Israel found in what became for Christians the Old Testament. They believed that those writings contained on virtually every page the promise of salvation destined to find fulfillment in Christ. As Paul himself says very attractively, "He [Jesus Christ] is the 'Yes' to all the promises of God" (2 Cor 1:20). This means that, in his letters to the communities of believers, Paul constantly presupposes and alludes to texts from the Old Testament and also to Jewish traditions drawn from the texts that he has communicated to his converts as part of their instruction in the faith. As has been widely recognized in Pauline scholarship in recent decades, Jewish traditions about Adam, drawn from the opening chapters of the Book of Genesis, played a significant role in this respect, notably in Paul's understanding of the redemptive role of Christ, whom he portrays as "New" or "Last [i.e., latter-day] Adam" (1 Cor 15:45b). Also particularly significant for Paul, as for the New Testament generally, was the final section of the Book of Isaiah (Isaiah 40—66), where a prophet ("Deutero-Isaiah") writing at the time of the Babylonian exile proclaimed the "good news" of freedom and return to the promised land (Isa 40:9; 52:7; 61:1). The early Christian believers understood this prophetic gospel as a "pre-announcement" of the liberation from sin and death they had experienced in Christ (Rom 1:1–2). All this means that it is necessary when considering Paul to take into account Old Testament texts that form a significant background to his own thought, in particular the early chapters of Genesis. Accordingly, this scriptural background will have its place in the material presented, especially in the early days of the retreat.

What about the Gospels, and especially episodes they record from the life and ministry of Jesus that have over the ages been particularly treasured as sources for contemplation during retreats? Because this is a Pauline retreat, scenes from the Gospels are rarely discussed. This does not mean, however, that the retreatant should not seek to relate what Paul is saying about Christ to favorite scenes in the Gospels where making such connection seems particularly apposite. As is now widely accepted in church teaching since the middle of the last century, the Gospels are written out of the Easter faith of the believing communities. The Jesus who features centrally in them is not just the Jesus of his pre-passion life but the risen and exalted Lord, carrying out his mission through the power of the Spirit. The early believers heard and read the stories in the Gospels not simply about "back there" in Palestine in the days of Jesus' historical life. They heard and read those stories as their stories too, as depicting who and what Jesus as risen Lord was for them in their own time and place. In this sense, the Jesus of the Gospels and the Jesus of Paul are identically the same person, on mission from the Father to live and die, in self-sacrificial love, for the life of the world. If readers and retreatants wish to take a comment about a Pauline passage to a gospel episode for contemplation and prayer, that is perfectly appropriate and indeed commendable. In fact, at the end of each reflection, there are some questions for prayerful consideration that point to other scriptural texts that seem particularly appropriate in each case, including the Gospels.

Along with the reflections, I have included translations of the texts that I am considering at that particular point. The Scripture translations draw on the New Revised Standard Version but are basically my own. In places, I do not hesitate to cite and discuss the underlying Greek word—always in transliteration. It is frequently necessary to do so in order that the full riches of Paul's thought—often masked in translation—may appear. I trust that such excursions will not deter the dedicated reader.

As stated previously, the reflections contained in this book fall into a schema of two a day for each of eight days. Despite this pattern, whether in the case of a "Do-it-yourself retreat" or a retreat under the guidance of a spiritual director or companion, there should be no need to adhere rigidly to the pattern or "get through" all the reflections in a set number of days. The Ignatian principle that in a retreat experience "it is not to know much, but it is to understand and savor the matter interiorly, that fills and satisfies the soul" (*Spiritual Exercises* §2 [Annotation 2]) should prevail. In the same vein, rather than moving on immediately from an exercise based on one reflection to the next, it may often help to repeat the prayer on the same matter, especially where the text has had a powerful appeal the first time around. What is essential in a retreat is the interaction between divine grace and the spiritual center ("soul") of the person making the retreat. The reflections presented here are simply external aids that may be taken up, postponed, or left aside as seems best at the time.

INTRODUCTION

Paul and Prayer

In a retreat setting, when a person is going to spend some time in actual converse with God, it helps to consider at an early stage Paul's own sense of prayer. He does not provide an explicit teaching on prayer; he simply presumes that prayer—both private and communal—will be a regular feature of Christian life:

> Rejoice always, pray without ceasing, give thanks in all circumstances; for this is the will of God in Christ Jesus for you. (1 Thess 5:16–18)

> Rejoice in hope, be patient in suffering, persevere in prayer. (Rom 12:12)

THANKSGIVING PRAYERS

Paul does, however, often allow his audience to "over-hear" his prayers. The introductory section of the letters regularly features an extended thanksgiving prayer recalling all the blessings the recipients have received since the beginning of their Christian life.[1] For much of its length, the Letter to the Ephesians is a sustained prayerful reflection on the divine work of bringing all things to a unity in Christ. The high point is an extended sequence at the close of chapter 3:

> For this reason I bow my knees before the Father, from whom every family in heaven and on earth takes its name. I pray that, according to the riches of his glory, he may grant that you may be strengthened in your inner being with power through his Spirit, and that Christ may dwell in your hearts through faith, as you are being rooted and grounded in love. I pray that you may have the power to comprehend, with all the saints, what is the breadth and length and height and depth, and to know the love of Christ that surpasses knowledge, so that you may be filled with all the fullness of God.
>
> Now to him who by the power at work within us is able to accomplish abundantly far more than all we can ask or imagine, to him be glory in the church and in Christ Jesus to all generations, forever and ever. Amen. (Eph 3:14–21)

Everyone beginning a retreat could make this prayer their own. It is hard to imagine a more adequate expression of the grace to be sought and obtained.

THE "GROANS" OF THE SPIRIT WITHIN (ROM 8:26–27)

Likewise, when beginning a retreat, it is helpful to be aware of a small passage where Paul draws attention to what is going on in the actual process of prayer. Recognizing that prayer can be difficult, Paul speaks of the Spirit's coming to the assistance of "our weakness":

> Likewise the Spirit helps us in our weakness; for when we do not know how we should pray [or what to pray for] that same Spirit intercedes with groans too deep for words. And God, who searches the heart, knows what is the mind of the Spirit, because the Spirit intercedes for the saints according to the will of God. (Rom 8:26–27)

The middle clause of verse 26 is normally translated "when we do not know *how* to pray." This means that "our weakness" consists primarily in a difficulty of knowing how to pray—an interpretation that has brought comfort to many, since prayer is an exercise of faith, often with little sensible consolation or felt presence of God. The actual Greek that Paul wrote (*ti*, rather than *pōs*) is more accurately translated "what to pray for." The weakness in question, then, would derive from our not being able to see or imagine the future that God has in store for us and hence not knowing what we are praying for. Although this latter interpretation adheres more closely to what Paul had in mind in the immediate context of Romans, the former remains the majority view. Exegetically speaking, you are in good company if you choose to adopt it.

So much for the problem—"our weakness"—what about "the groans too deep for words" with which the Spirit comes to our aid when we pray? "Too deep for words" is an attractive translation of the Greek adjective *alalētos*, which means "unable to be spoken" or "unable to be expressed in words." The thought seems to be that the Spirit prays within us at a level that is below the level of our consciousness—so deep that we cannot "hear" this intercession of the Spirit, let alone ourselves give utterance to it in thought or words.

At the risk of taking the passage somewhat out of context, we can find here something very helpful for our prayer. As Paul writes earlier in Romans, "God's love has been poured out into our hearts through the Holy Spirit that has been given to us" (5:5). The Spirit takes us into the communion of love that is the Trinity (though, of course, such a way of describing God emerged well after Paul). Prayer is not, then, something in which we have to be always active, always "making conversation" with God. There are times, perhaps most of the time, when we should just try to be still, confident that the Holy Spirit is praying to the Father in the depths of our hearts, even though we cannot feel or sense that at the time.

After all, the whole mission of Christ, as presented in the Gospels is intended to draw us into the communion of love that is the Trinity. All three Synoptic Gospels preface the beginning of Jesus' ministry with a description of what he experiences as he emerges from the water in which he has received baptism from John: the Spirit comes down upon him in the form of a dove, and he hears the voice of the Father: "You are my Son, the beloved, my favor rests on you" (see Matt 3:16–17; Mark 1:9–11; Luke 3:21–22; also see John 1:32–34). This sense of being loved by the Father communicated in the Spirit will be the engine of Jesus' ministry to follow—a ministry in which he will seek to draw all people into that same communion of love. This is essentially what Paul wishes to express in the "triune" grace with which he concludes 2 Corinthians:

Introduction

The grace of the Lord Jesus Christ, the love of God
[the Father] and the communion of the Holy Spirit
be with you all. (13:13)

A well-known spiritual writer maintains that the reason
that so many people fail to make progress in the spiritual
life is that they simply won't sit still and let God love them.[2]
Prayer is so often simply a time of trying to sit still under that
canopy of love.

"WHAT ARE YOU DOING HERE, ELIJAH?" (1 KGS 19:1-16)

Scripture offers many texts suitable for the beginning of a retreat. The Elijah cycle recorded in 1 Kings 19:1–16 is particularly apt in this regard. Paul too, at one point in his Letter to the Romans (11:2–6), identifies with a lament made by the prophet to God. For that reason, too, it is appropriate to consider this passage.

At this moment in his troubled prophetic career, Elijah is isolated and in danger of his life. The kingdom is in the hands of the weak king, Ahab, largely ruled by his wife, Jezebel, who has become the prophet's deadly enemy. Hearing that Ahab, at the behest of Jezebel, had killed all the prophets with the sword and has in mind a similar fate for him, Elijah flees for his life to Beersheba in the southernmost region of Judah (1 Kgs 19:1–3).

Going a day's journey further into the wilderness, Elijah sits down under a solitary broom tree and asks that he might die. "It is enough, Lord, take away my life, for I am no better than my ancestors" (v. 4). We have here a perfect biblical picture of depression: Elijah is exhausted, utterly disillusioned, his mission seemingly at the end, and his companions slain. He lies down under the broom tree and falls asleep.

But not for long! Suddenly an angel is waking him and telling him to get up and eat. Elijah wakes up and finds a cake baked on hot stones and a jar of water at his head. He eats and drinks, and then promptly goes back to sleep. Such a human touch: refreshed by the food and drink, Elijah simply goes back to sleep (v. 6)—like someone switching off the alarm instead of getting out of bed. Angels on mission, however, are not so easily put off. Again Elijah is awoken with the instruction to "eat, lest the journey will be too much for you" (v. 7). So the Lord has a journey in store for Elijah. The food is sustenance for that journey.

Strengthened by that food and drink, Elijah walks forty days and forty nights into the wilderness until he comes to Horeb, the mountain of God. *Horeb* is an alternative name for Sinai, the scene of Israel's encounter with God following the exodus from Egypt. Elijah is journeying to the locale of his people's foundational experience of God, where Israel entered into the covenant with God that was to define her identity and regulate her vocation as people of God. Here, at Horeb-Sinai, he will experience God anew, this time in a deeply personal way.

Elijah spends the night in a cave (v. 9a). In the morning (presumably), the word of the Lord comes to him with the question, "What are you doing here, Elijah? (v. 9b). Elijah makes his complaint, tells it as it is: "I have been very zealous for the Lord, the God of hosts, for the Israelites have forsaken your covenant, thrown down your altars, and killed your prophets with the sword. I alone am left, and they are seeking my life to take it away" (v. 10; see Rom 11:2–3).

In response, Elijah receives the instruction to go out (from the cave) and stand upon the mountain before the Lord (v. 11). The reason is that the Lord is "about to pass by." "Pass by" is technical biblical language indicating that a revelation of God (theophany) is about to take place.[1] Here, the divine "passing by" occurs in one of the most mysterious episodes in the entire biblical tradition. There came "a great wind, so strong that it was splitting the mountains and breaking the rocks in pieces before the Lord," but the Lord was not in the wind; after the wind an earthquake, but the Lord was not in the earthquake (v. 11), and after the earthquake, a fire (perhaps lightning is meant), but the Lord was not in the fire. Following all these violent manifestations of nature that the Lord was not "in," there came "a sound of sheer silence" (v. 12). This last phrase, with its seemingly contradictory elements of both "sound" and "silence," has tantalized interpreters and translators for centuries. The traditional English translation (KJV) "still small voice" has never lost its appeal. The NRSV "a sound of sheer silence" is also an attractive option. My sense of the Hebrew and the context (following the mighty wind, the splitting of the rocks, the earthquake, and so on) is that what is meant is something that combines both "stillness" and "silence." I would suggest "a sound of silent stillness."[2] The overall sense is that, after the noise created by the earthquake, the rock-splitting wind, and the lightning, the sensation of gentle calm is so palpable as to be virtually audible. (City dwellers, living among constant noise from traffic, often experience the silence of the countryside as an audible "absence" of sound.) It is probably impossible to recover the original meaning of the phrase with any degree of certainty. That is not a loss, however. We are left with a richly evocative ambiguity that can go in many directions.

However, the contrast being made in regard to the revelation of God is clear. The violent wind, the earthquake, and the fire evoke the terrifying manifestation of the divine presence that Israel experienced in this same locale (before Mount Sinai) following the exodus (Exod 19:16–25; Deut 4:10–12; 5:2–5, 25–31). What Elijah now experiences is so different, so much more gentle, inward, and silent. This is a great moment in the religious tradition of Israel. The God previously known in remote and fearsome splendor is now heard in stillness and peace.

So Elijah goes out and stands at the entrance of his cave (v. 13a). He hears the same question as before, "What are you doing here, Elijah?" (v. 13b) and, in response, repeats his earlier protest and lament (v. 14; see v. 10). The response does not suggest that he has been greatly changed by what he has experienced on the mountain. Whatever the case, he is immediately given a new mission: to anoint two kings, one for Aram, one for Israel (v. 15), and to anoint Elisha as prophet in his place (v. 16). From being an exhausted, utterly disillusioned prophet who simply wants to die (v. 5), his journey to the place of his people's original encounter with God and his experience of that encounter in a deeply personal way has renewed his spirit and set him upon a fresh stage of prophetic mission (1 Kgs 19:19–21; 21:17–29; 2 Kgs 2:1–13).

In several respects, this experience of Elijah can speak to people setting out on a retreat. Many come from busy lives, able, with all due allowance for God's grace, to make the prophet's words their own: "I have been very zealous for the Lord of hosts." Many may feel exhausted, disillusioned even, by the experience of working in demanding and difficult roles. A retreat is a time of going, to some degree, "into the wilderness"—on a personal journey into the heart of one's experience of God. It is good to hear that question twice put by God to Elijah addressed by name to ourselves, "What are you doing here…?" and to ponder prayerfully the various ways in which we might respond. Finally, we might hope that, as in the case of Elijah, a renewed sense of mission might be the outcome of our experience of God in retreat.

"What are you doing here, Elijah?"

PERSONAL REFLECTION

After reading the passage (1 Kgs 19:1–16) prayerfully, are
    there aspects of the story with which I can identify?
As I begin this retreat, I hear the Lord ask me, "What are you
    doing here, [*name*]?" How do I respond?
What is the *deepest* level at which I can respond to the
    question?
Ask the Lord to reveal over the coming days what his will is
    that I should learn:
        about God,
        about myself,
        about the mission to which he is now sending me.

PRAYER

Lord, reveal yourself to me.
Lord, let me know what you wish me to know.
Lord, lead me now to where you wish to meet me.

DAY 1

THE GIFT OF CREATION

St. Ignatius begins the *Spiritual Exercises* by placing the person who makes them in the context of the whole of creation. Within the vision of faith that he presupposes, human beings are not purely autonomous but have life and indeed existence through the gift of One who is not created, namely God. Like a bedrock foundation for the retreat, Ignatius wants to establish this sense of being in relation to God as creature to Creator, and to draw all other relationships that we have as human beings within the ambit of this fundamental relationship with God.

To experience our creatureliness is an important fruit of the retreat. This is not so easy in the world in which most of us live—an urban environment where we are surrounded and constantly served by what we human beings have made. We are not so close to nature as on a rural property or when we go bushwalking, camping, and so on. For good and for ill, we are insulated in so many ways from the direct impact of the natural world. As the Jesuit poet Gerard Manley Hopkins put it over a century ago:

> Generations have trod, have, have trod;
> And all is seared with trade; bleared, smeared with toil;

And wears man's smudge and shares man's smell:
   the soil
Is bare now, nor can foot feel, being shod.[1]

The Bible presupposes our creaturehood from beginning to end, establishing this truth intentionally and explicitly at its very beginning, in the Creation stories of Genesis 1—3. These opening chapters of the Bible were very important for Paul as well. It is true to say that he saw that what God was doing in the life and ministry of Christ amounted to a rewriting of the story of Creation. Or—to put it perhaps more accurately—in Christ, God was bringing the original project of Creation to realization for the first time. One of Paul's more memorable catchphrases runs, "If anyone is in Christ, behold a new creation" (2 Cor 5:17). To be baptized is to enter into the sphere of the new creation, the coming true at last of God's design for human beings and the world, so much of which has been thwarted by sin. In this early stage of the retreat, it is helpful to linger for some time on these early chapters of the Bible that Paul reclaimed for his own work as agent of the gospel.

THE FIRST ACCOUNT OF CREATION (GEN 1:1—2:3)

First, we have to be clear that creation is not about "back there"—about the origins of the universe. Nowadays, we go to science to learn about that. The biblical understanding of creation is about now. It's about a vision of ourselves and our world as the gift of God. The account of Creation, contained in the first chapter of Genesis and trespassing a little into the second, does not provide a literal description of how various elements of the universe and living creatures came into being. It does narrate that process in a poetic way and according to the understanding of the time. It does so, however, not to give information about origins but to communicate an attitude to the world that is as valid for our time as it was for its original audience. It is communicating the sense that everything on the face of the earth is not just there of its own accord nor is it simply the product of impersonal natural forces. Everything is, in some sense, the gift of God and enters into human relationship with God. Everything emerging from the divine hand is declared "good." If evil has entered the world—and that is an issue the Book of Genesis will deal with very soon—such evil is not an inherent or necessary element in anything that God has made.

Worthy of particular note is the divine deliberation that precedes the creation of human beings: "Let us make humankind in our own image, according to our likeness" (1:26a). In the understanding of the original text, God is speaking to other heavenly beings, reflecting the ancient idea of a heavenly community or court of divine beings (Job 1; Ps 82; Isa 6). The motivation for Creation is not because God is lonely in the universe. Rather, Creation involves a desire on God's part to deepen and broaden the community of relationships that already exists in the divine realm.[2] Going well beyond the purview of the story in Genesis, reading it in the light of our Christian faith, we can find here a hint of the Trinity as a communion of love between divine persons. The act of Creation would then represent a divine desire to extend that love more widely—or rather to draw other beings into that community of love, since love is always selflessly expansive.

To this end, God creates human beings in the divine image and likeness (1:26–28), that is, as persons able to respond in love, a response that of course requires freedom. Creating personal beings, rather than puppets or robots subject to control, involves the risk that something other than love will be forthcoming. The account will soon go on to explore this risk of freedom.

At the gates of cities in the ancient world, it was customary to set up images of the local ruler or of the distant emperor to ensure that all those entering would know whose writ ran in the place and behave accordingly. Creation in the divine image and likeness probably has something to do with this practice. God sets up human beings as "viceroys" in the world, to image and extend divine dominion over the earth. Implied is responsibility for the rest of creation, with a care and concern for its most vulnerable elements on the model of the kind of dominion expected of a good Israelite king (see, e.g., Ps 72:8–14). There is, however, the risk that human preeminence of this kind will result, not in responsible stewardship, but exploitation.

Today, many people, from an ecological standpoint, have strong reservations about this anthropocentric view emerging from the first account of Creation.[3] It is difficult to get around the fact that the text does accord human beings a central and indeed dominant role vis-à-vis other beings on the face of the earth. (Besides Genesis 1:26–28, Psalm 8 offers a more poetic view of the same human centrality.) But this surely reflects the actual situation where humans, for good and for ill, do call the shots in the world—increasingly so as technology develops.[4] Moreover, the Creation story does not assign human beings a special "day" to themselves, but places us along with other living beings in the final sixth day of God's creative work (Gen 1:24–31). This communicates the sense of all, humans and other living creatures, being bound together, in a community of life that is dubbed not just "good" but "very good" (v. 31).

It is "good" but it is not perfect. The waters of chaos that God pushed away and confined to create the dry land (1:6–10) remain. They will return in the flood story (6:5—8:22), where

10

creation seems to go into reverse, as human sinfulness and violence spreads over the earth. So Creation remains a "work in progress," with human beings given a principal role—for good and for ill. We will return to this later when considering Paul's sense of the duel between the "sin" story of the human race told in Adam and the "grace" story told in Christ.

In conclusion, though, as we leave the first Creation story, let us note the attractively "human" way in which the account depicts God as a creative artist, working over a six-day week and then taking a rest on the seventh day (2:2). Even more attractive is the contemplative mode in which the account constantly depicts God: sitting back, as it were, after the work of each day, viewing the result, and seeing it all as "good." The account, then, when we read or pray over it, invites us into this divine contemplation. Or, to put it the other way around, to understand that when we attempt to enter into a contemplative mode in prayer or, even better, feel ourselves drawn into such a mode by something beautiful or attractive that arrests us, we are being drawn into God's own contemplation of the work of creation.

THE SECOND ACCOUNT OF CREATION (GEN 2:4—3:24)

When we turn to the second account of Creation in Genesis 2 and 3, we encounter something quite different. Here, although the remainder of creation is not absent—notably the animals that the man names (2:19–20)—the central focus is on the creation of human beings and the relationship between them and the Creator that follows.

The account begins (2:5) with the image of the earth as a dry desert or wilderness—no plants or grass. In biblical tradition, the wilderness often functions as an image for a frightening place of evil and death. God's creative activity here will

11

be to turn the wilderness into a garden of life. What is needed is water and someone to till the ground. A stream arises from under the ground to provide water; so that need is solved. Operating like a master potter, God provides for the second by shaping man from the dust of the earth (2:7a).[5] Going beyond what a human potter could do, God breathes into the clay model the breath of life, so that the man becomes a living being (2:7b). The effect is to portray life as a divine gift; every breath we take is a reminder of the giftedness of life.[6] Our life flows from the breath of God. (The word *breath* in Hebrew, *ruach*, also serves for "wind" and "spirit.") The gift of the Spirit, then, will be a continuation of this life-giving, creative gift of God—as in the popular hymn to the Holy Spirit, "O Breathe on Me, O Breath of God."

Having created the man in this way, God plants in Eden (v. 8) a lush garden of beauty and goodness for him to till. Two trees in particular stand in the garden: the tree of life and the tree of the knowledge of good and evil. These trees will play a significant role later in the story. We may let them be for the moment. For the present, let us note that the garden is not a vacation resort for the man but a workplace in which he has a vocation: to "till and keep" the garden (v. 15). There is, then, responsibility: a shared responsibility with God to care for the earth and ensure that it remains a garden. There is also freedom: freedom, arising out of divine generosity, to enjoy the fruits of the garden: "You may freely eat of every tree of the garden" (v. 16). But there is one limiting prohibition: "But of the tree of the knowledge of good and evil you shall not eat, for in the day that you eat of it you shall die" (v. 17).

What is meant or symbolized by "the tree of the knowledge of good and evil" has eluded satisfactory explanation. Most interpreters seem to agree that the prohibition at least expresses the limit of human existence, human creatureliness.

Belief in God acknowledges that God is God and human beings are not God but beings who have received the gift of life and existence from One who alone can bestow it.[7] When human beings seek to go beyond the limits of creatureliness, when they claim complete autonomy, they are acting as if God did not exist. By creating and entering into relationship with human beings, God is, in fact, drawing them into the divine, eternal life. But such divinization of the human is a gift from God. It cannot be grasped or grabbed aside from God. Human beings can only become "divine," realize the full potential of being created in the divine likeness, through a life-long process of learning how to love. To be drawn in this way into the divine communion of love that is the Trinity is to share God's own eternal life.

In connection, we may say, with love, God realizes that something is lacking in the human life that has been created: "It is not good that man should be alone" (2:18). The man needs someone to love and to be loved by; he needs a companion—or, as the text puts it literally, "a helper."[8]

True to the bond already established by the creation of all living beings on a single day (1:24–31), God parades the animals before the man, inviting him to name them. None of them, however, satisfies the human longing for companionship. So God adopts a different strategy, creating woman out of the man's rib while he sleeps (2:21–22). When the man awakes, there is immediate recognition that this is truly the companion for whom he had been yearning: "This at last is bone of my bone and flesh of my flesh" (2:23). Although the woman is created in this "derivative" way from the man, there is no suggestion of inferiority; on the contrary, the qualities emerging from the text are those of companionship, complementarity, and equality. There is not even the sense that the union is primarily for procreation. The stress is entirely on relationship: the man is to leave the most significant relationship in his life hitherto—that with his father and mother; primary from now on will be this new companionship with the woman (2:24). Moreover, the final remark that they were naked and knew no shame (2:25) underlines intimacy: a physical intimacy as between man and wife in sexual union, but more deeply an emotional intimacy of love and trust, with no barriers between them.

On this note of intimacy, God's work of Creation as told in the second account ends. There is intimacy between God and the human beings he has created—an intimacy that will emerge as an issue in the story to follow. There is a "horizontal" intimacy between the human pair. There is, in a sense, even a close relationship—though hardly intimacy—between the human pair and the animal world that they have "named."

REFLECTION

If we reflect on the image of God as Creator that emerges from these first two chapters of Genesis, there is certainly the sense—emerging particularly from the first Creation story—of the transcendence of God, of the divine "otherness" from all creatures. This is balanced by the sense—emerging especially, though not exclusively, from the second account—of God in close relationship with creatures, especially human beings. "The realm of the divine and the realm of the creature are not radically unrelated spheres; there are overlapping powers, roles, and responsibilities."[9] God leaves room, so to speak, for decisions on the part of human beings—even decisions that are dangerous and destructive. As we are more conscious today, the future of the world, for good and for ill, stands so much within our hands (think: exchange of nuclear weaponry; ecological devastation). The doctrine of Creation does not necessarily mean that, like parents of a spoiled child, God will "fix up" the world for us, no matter how destructively we behave. Nonetheless, God is shown in Genesis as already having to make adjustments in the divine will for the world in the light of human decisions and behavior. As the social philosopher Charles Taylor has said, "God is like a skilled tennis player, who can always return the serve."[10] Divine sovereignty in creation, therefore, does not mean absolute divine control. God can only relate to human beings in a personal way on the basis of freedom. That means taking the risk of sharing with us, for good and for ill, responsibility and power over creation.

St. Ignatius did not explicitly draw on or cite the biblical texts in drawing up the "First Principle and Foundation," which he placed at the head of the *Spiritual Exercises*. He does, however, seem to have intended that, at the beginning of the retreat, retreatants place themselves within a vision of God that is basically the same as the one emerging from the opening chapters of the Bible. Common to both is the sense of human beings as creatures, yet free to make decisions and relate to other creatures within that vision of the Godhead. Where Ignatius can perhaps be faulted is in a failure to distinguish "all other creatures" (aside from "myself" and God), lumping together human beings, animals, and inanimate objects. Surely, my relationship to other human beings is of a different order from my relationship with my house, my car, my iPad, or other possessions. What Ignatius does emphasize, above all, is that the relationship with God is paramount, and all other relationships must be ordered within it. That is what he means by "saving one's soul," since "soul" is that aspect of our person where we relate to God above all. Drawing to Ignatius the more comprehensive vision stemming from the early chapters of the Bible, we can find a special place for our human relationships—aware, that, in many respects, we go to God and find God, not aside from or around but precisely in and through our deepest and most intimate relationships with other people. Let us allow God to draw us more deeply into this creaturely relationship, the sure foundation of an Ignatian retreat.

SUGGESTED SCRIPTURE

Psalms 8; 102 (103); 144 (145); Job 38; Isaiah 40:12–31; 45:18–25; 55:1–13; 65:17—66:2

PERSONAL REFLECTION

Take some time to sit consciously within the loving embrace of the God who made you:

> We were conceived in the heart of God and for this reason "each of us is the result of a thought of God. Each of us is willed, each of us is loved, each of us is necessary" (Pope Francis, *Laudato Si'* 65 [citing Pope Benedict XVI]).

Consider all my relationships with other human beings, especially those that are most close and intimate, within this overall relationship with God.

Consider all the benefits I have received throughout my life and continue to receive as the gift of God rather than as things simply taken for granted.

What relationships, in particular, lead me to God and reflect God's love for me? Are there any that, on the contrary, distance me from God or do not sit easily within that basic relationship?

Likewise, what gifts or possessions seem particularly to lead me to God? Are there any that, on the contrary, get in the way?

CREATED IN LOVE

A feature of the New Testament that merits more attention than it regularly receives finds a role for Christ in the biblical story of Creation. We can easily slip into thinking that Christ came along to do a kind of repair job on creation gone awry. Several important New Testament documents, however, see Christ there "in the beginning," right from the start. In other words, creation, no less than redemption, is all about Christ.

Perhaps the most familiar statement to this effect comes at the start of the Fourth Gospel:

> In the beginning was the Word, and the Word was with God, and the Word was God. This was in the beginning with God. Through him all things came to be, and apart from him there came to be not a single thing of all that has come to be. (John 1:1–3)

According to the account of Creation in Genesis 1, the very first act on God's part was the creation of light. This came about as God said, "Let there be light" (Gen 1:3). The Fourth Gospel at its very beginning personifies this creative word ("Let there be" [one word in Hebrew]). As the Prologue unfolds, what emerges is that the creative Word God spoke—and continues to speak—is God's eternal Son who took flesh in the person of Jesus Christ (1:14). In other words, the Gospel presents Jesus Christ as God's creative Word. Wherever he speaks or acts in the story, it is God saying, "Let there be…": "Let there be life," "Let there be light."[11] This communicates not so much that Christ was "back there" at creation, but that creation is continuing and indeed coming to fulfillment in the work of Christ. Seeing everything in the light of Christ, the evangelist has drawn creation to Christ and presented him as simply "the fullness (*plērōma*) of [God's] grace and truth" (John 1:14, 16), as distinct from a more partial foreshadowing of such fullness in previous gifts of God.[12]

It is generally agreed that, in relating Christ to creation, the Fourth Gospel is drawing on the Wisdom tradition of Israel, especially as seen in Proverbs 8:22–31. In Paul's letters, we find traces of a similar connection between the Wisdom tradition and the person and work of Christ. In 1 Corinthians, Paul responds to a query from the community at Corinth as to whether it was lawful for them to eat meat left over from sacrifices in pagan temples. Citing what appears to be a snatch of an early creed, he dismisses the reality of any divine being apart from the God of Christian faith and worship:

> Indeed, even though there may be so-called gods in heaven or on earth—as in fact there are many gods and many lords—yet for us there is one God, the Father, from whom are all things and for whom [literally, "unto whom"] we exist, and one Lord, Jesus Christ, through whom are all things and through whom we exist. (1 Cor 8:5–6)

The balanced formula beginning "yet for us" neatly sums up the notion of God (the Father) as ultimate origin and destiny of human beings, and of Christ as the instrument whereby we come into being and achieve that destiny (eternal life with God). Happily for us, Paul is incapable of addressing any issue, no matter how commonplace, without drawing on rich reserves of theology such as we find here. The little creed aptly communicates the idea of human life, encapsulated from beginning to end within the creative design of the Father, unfolding and being realized in Christ.

CHRIST, THE WISDOM OF GOD (COL 1:13–20)

A more developed reworking of the Wisdom tradition of Israel appears early in the Letter to the Colossians. In the introduction to the letter, Paul gives thanks to the Father "who has enabled you to share in the inheritance of the saints in the light" (1:12) and continues:

> He has rescued us from the power of darkness and transferred us into the kingdom of his beloved Son, in whom we have redemption, the forgiveness of sins. (vv. 13–14)

After this allusion to the redemptive work of Christ, there follows a quotation from what seems to be an early Christian hymn. The hymn celebrates Christ's role in creation (vv. 15–17) before aspects of redemption come to fore once again (vv. 18–20):

> He is the image of the invisible God, the firstborn of all creation; for in him all things in heaven and earth were created, things visible and invisible, whether thrones or dominions or rulers or powers—all things have been created for him. He himself is before all things, and in him all things hold together.

As "image of the invisible God," Christ is the manifestation of God in the universe,[13] assuming as such the role conferred on human beings at the Creation (Gen 1:26–28). "Firstborn" (*prōtotokos*) has the meaning not only of priority but also of rule. Christ is "before" all other creatures because he is instrumental in their creation; by the same token, he is or is destined to be sovereign over all creatures. They have been created "for him" in the sense that he is not merely the *origin* but also the *goal* of creation. All creatures find the true

19

meaning of their existence in so far as they come under his liberating rule. All things "hold together in him" (v. 17) in that, aside from his rule, creation would revert to the original conflict, fragmentation, and chaos (Gen 1:2).

While the scope of the hymn extends to all creatures without exception, particularly in view, as indicated by the reference to "thrones, dominions, rulers and powers," are the forces—spiritual and worldly—that have influence and control over human affairs, whether for good or ill but chiefly for ill. As stated in the sentence that introduces the hymn, God has "rescued us from the power of darkness and transferred us into the kingdom of his beloved Son" (v. 13). God has initiated the process whereby the setup of the universe envisaged in Creation (vv. 14–16) will be brought to realization in, through, and for Christ. Once again we can see here that creation and redemption are not really envisaged as separate divine acts but opposite sides of the same coin, redemption overcoming "blockages" to creation's full realization according to the original plan of God.

In its second stanza, the hymn moves from creation to redemption:

> [Christ] is the head of the body, the church; he is the beginning, the firstborn from the dead, so that he might come to have first place in everything. For in him all the fullness [*plērōma*] of God was pleased to dwell, and through him God was pleased to reconcile to himself all things, whether on earth or in heaven, making peace through the blood of his cross. (vv. 18–20)

The introduction of Christ's supremacy over the church ("the body") follows somewhat abruptly upon his role in creation. Nonetheless, the motifs we would associate more naturally with redemption (the church, resurrection, reconciliation) are perfectly continuous with the divine work of creation. The "filling" of the universe expressed in the Greek word *plērōma* (v. 19) is a biblical way of expressing the extension of God's power and authority throughout the cosmos. Christ is the supreme location and instrument of this divine "filling," overcoming the hostility toward God through his reconciling and "peace-making" death (v. 20), and then, as risen Lord (see v. 18), continuing and extending the "filling" through the church which is his body. The sense appears to be that creation cannot arrive at its full goal without the reconciling work of Christ overcoming the hostility that has thwarted and continues to thwart God's gift of life and love to the world.

Thus, like the Prologue of the Fourth Gospel, the hymn cited by Paul in Colossians fills out the vision of Creation in Genesis by finding there a central role for Christ. As image of God (1:15; also see 2 Cor 4:4–6; Rom 8:29), Christ successfully replays the role in the new creation that Adam representatively "muffed" in the old. We can think of creation as the divine making of something out of nothing—an understanding of the divine activity not lacking in the New Testament (e.g., Rom 4:17). However, biblical thought perhaps more characteristically conceives of Creation as bringing about order and beauty where chaos and disorder had hitherto prevailed (the "formless void and darkness" of Gen 1:2), the overcoming of darkness by light (Gen 1:3–5). This biblical understanding of God's creative activity was congenial to finding a place for Christ and his redemptive role within the divine work of bringing creation to its intended goal. Therefore, at the beginning of a retreat when we place ourselves within this scope of creation, we are also placing ourselves in the deepest union with the person and work of Christ.

Once again, the Jesuit poet Gerard Manley Hopkins has put it so well in his sonnet: "As Kingfishers Catch Fire":

As kingfishers catch fire, dragonflies draw flame;
As tumbled over rim in roundy wells
Stones ring; like each tucked string tells, each hung
    bell's
Bow swung finds tongue to fling out broad its name;
Each mortal thing does one thing and the same:
Deals out that being indoors each one dwells;
Selves—goes itself; *myself* it speaks and spells,
Crying *Whát I dó is me: for that I came.*

I say móre: the just man justices;
Keeps grace: thát keeps all his goings graces;
Acts in God's eye what in God's eye he is—
Christ—for Christ plays in ten thousand places,
Lovely in limbs, and lovely in eyes not his
To the Father through the features of men's faces.[14]

IN PRAISE OF GOD'S PLAN TO UNIFY ALL THINGS IN CHRIST (EPH 1:3–14)

Most scholars agree that, while Colossians has been composed either directly by Paul or by a coworker at his instigation, the Letter to the Ephesians is the product of a later writer, who drew on the model provided by Colossians to provide instruction in Paul's name. Ephesians may not, then, be directly from Paul. Nonetheless, it does provide a superb distillation of his theology and sense of apostolic vocation. We should have no difficulty in hearing Paul speak to us through the letter—as has, of course, been the constant practice of the church through the ages.

Having considered the place of Christ in creation as presented in the opening hymn in Colossians, let us now recall the similar hymn or, rather, psalm of blessing that occurs in the introduction to Ephesians (1:3–14). This is even more apt, given that central to the psalm of blessing is the praise of God: "the praise of [God's] glory" (1:12, 14) or "the praise of the glory of God's grace" (1:6). Those familiar with the *Spiritual Exercises* will be aware that St. Ignatius prefaces the entire document with the "First Principle and Foundation," which begins, "Man [*sic*] was created to *praise*, reverence, and serve God our Lord and by this means to save his [*sic*] soul" (§23). The blessing psalm heading Ephesians sweeps us up into this attitude of reverence and praise.

What associations does the word "praise" stir up within us? Praise can, of course, be insincere and self-seeking, moving in the direction of flattery. Sincere praise, however, is a selfless acknowledgment of the achievement, the beauty, or the quality of another. When directed toward God, praise also incorporates strong notes of thanksgiving, admiration, and awe. It is interesting that Paul in 2 Corinthians speaks of his apostolic mission in these terms: "Yes, everything is for your sake, so that grace, as it extends to more and more people, may increase thanksgiving, to the glory of God" (4:15). The single sentence, almost a throwaway remark, suggests that the entire purpose of his mission, as an instrument of God's grace, is to multiply human gratitude to God across the world. The suggestion that this is ultimately and simply what God wants from human beings coheres very closely with what Ignatius has written in the first sentence of the "First Principle and Foundation": that human beings attain the end for which they have been created by letting this fundamental attitude of praise of God enclose, shape, and direct all their activity and all other attachments.

The blessing psalm making up Ephesians 1:3–14 consists of one long continuous sentence in the Greek original, with multiple tacked-on participial phrases and relative clauses. Modern English translations understandably break it down to render it more readable. In a retreat situation, however, it is good to know that the psalm seeks to gather the believer into the overwhelming paean of praise to God that it unfolds at such length.

Very prominent at the beginning and recurring again and again is the notion of divine choice ("election") and predestination in our regard. This is predestination in a wholly positive sense: prior to Creation, God has a plan or purpose (*thelēma*) in our regard (v. 3). The plan is that we should be "holy and blameless before him in love" (v. 4), God having "predestined" (*proorisas*) us to have the status of sons and daughters (*eis huiothesian*) "through Jesus Christ" (v. 5). In other words, God's whole prior intent in our regard is that our entire existence should be enveloped by divine love as children growing up within the security and freedom of a loving family.[15] It is all "through Christ Jesus" in that Christ is both instrument and model of humanity's attaining this end: our arrival "at the measure of the full stature of Christ" (4:13).

In light of this divine intent, the blessing psalm extolls the grace of God, literally, "to the praise of the glory of [God's] grace [*charis*] with which he graced us [*echaritōsen*] in the Beloved" (v. 6). "Grace" (*charis*) is, of course, a characteristic Pauline term. Its most basic meaning is that of "gift," and then, especially in the biblical tradition, it denotes the unmerited, totally gratuitous divine favor that lies behind and finds expression in all the gifts freely bestowed on us by God. While creation and all that goes with it is the basic *charis* of God, no less an expression, especially in view of the supreme cost involved, is the gift of redemption, which entailed "the giving up" on God's part of the beloved Son in order to free us from the burden of our sins. This manifests the "richness" of God's grace (v. 7b).

The ultimate intent of the Father "in the fullness of time" is "to sum up (*anakephalaiousthai*) all things in Christ" (v. 10). This highly suggestive phrase holds together the sense of drawing all things into a unity in Christ and doing so through the extension of Christ's lordship throughout the world. First Corinthians 15:20–28 portrays this extension of Christ's rule (on behalf of God) as a "program" still underway; the final stanza of the Christ hymn in Philippians 2:6–11 (vv. 9–11), in more liturgical mode, depicts it as already accomplished. We will return to both these Pauline passages later in the retreat.

The remainder of the blessing psalm (vv. 11–14) sees humanity drawn into the divine "economy" (*economia* [v. 10]) of salvation under the two ethnic categories basic to Paul and Jewish thought generally: the Jewish people ("we") and the remainder of the world ("Gentiles"). The divine plan was that "we" (Jews) should be the first to set our hope on Christ (vv. 11–12), while "you" (Gentiles), having believed in the "word of truth" that is the gospel, should come to be marked with the "seal of the Spirit," that is the pledge (literally, "down payment" [*arrabōn*]) of "the inheritance" promised to God's people (vv. 13–14). The Jewish people have been God's special "possession" since the exodus from Egypt. Now the presence of the Spirit in the communities of believers from the nations shows that they too have been drawn into the intimate filial relationship with God long since enjoyed by Israel (see Rom 8:15; Gal 4:6–7). The fullness of salvation may still be outstanding, but the Spirit guarantees that believers already enjoy the relationship with God characteristic of the final age.

The mention of the Spirit in the final stage of the blessing hymn introduces a trinitarian note that often emerges in the writings of Paul. Paul does not, of course, have a fully developed doctrine of the Trinity, but he does seem to think of the Godhead as a communion of love into which it is the divine will to draw human beings. The Spirit communicates to believers a sense of being swept up into that divine love, with the hope that it also entails. As Paul says in a wonderful sentence in Romans, "And hope will not let us down because God's love has been poured out into our hearts through the Holy Spirit that has been given us" (5:5).

On the human side, the response that is to be drawn forth from both categories of believers (Jewish and Gentile) is simply that of praising God for his glory (vv. 12 and 14). So the hymn ends where it began, seeking to draw us into a fundamental disposition of praise stemming from our knowledge of the divine "economy" of salvation that we have come to share through the gospel.

PERSONAL REFLECTION

Allow a prayerful reflection of these two hymns—at the beginning of Colossians and Ephesians, respectively—to draw you into a deeper awareness of being enveloped by the loving design of God. This will hopefully bring about a sense of praise appropriate for this time of retreat. In this context, it may be appropriate to revisit the questions that concluded the first reflection for today. A later passage in Colossians may also assist in this regard:

> Let the word of Christ dwell in you richly; teach and admonish one another in all wisdom; and with gratitude in your hearts sing psalms, hymns, and spiritual songs to God. And whatever you do, in word or deed, do everything in the name of the Lord Jesus, giving thanks to God the Father through him. (3:16–17)

DAY 2

LOST INTIMACY

The third chapter of the Book of Genesis features prominently in Paul's view of what God was doing for the world in Christ. So we will now spend some time on this chapter and on the loss of intimacy—in all directions—that it describes in mythological terms. Despite popular usage, *myth* in this context doesn't mean something that isn't true. On the contrary, it refers to something that, while not true in a literal, historical sense, is saying something so profoundly true about God and about human beings that it can only be told through story and symbol.

The mythical aspect is very much evident when, at the beginning of chapter 3, a new character, the serpent, appears on the scene. This is the only place—apart from the story of Balaam's ass in Numbers (22:27–30)—where an animal talks in the Bible! With this talking snake, we are in the realm of symbol and myth more than anywhere else in Scripture.

What does the serpent, as symbol, represent? That question has long been debated. We needn't go into the debate. The serpent, in fact, isn't the main focus of the text. What is central is the way in which the serpent suggests to the couple all the possibilities that are open to them in view of their placement in the garden and the freedom that they, uniquely among all other creatures, enjoy. In particular, the serpent serves to focus attention on the aspect of "limit" presented by the prohibition against eating the fruit of one tree: the tree of the knowledge of good and evil (2:16–17). The serpent is introduced from the start as more "crafty" than any other wild animal that the Lord had made (3:1). A recent tendency among Old Testament scholars has been to rehabilitate the serpent and suggest that it was clever, yes, but not malicious. I'm not so sure. The translation "crafty" (Hebrew, *arum*) rightly catches the sense that the serpent is up to no good— that it wants in some way to undermine the relationship between God and the human couple. It shows its craftiness by drawing attention to a sensitive area: the one limitation on freedom that the prohibition concerning the fruit of this tree represents. The couple have complete freedom to enjoy the fruits of the garden in all other respects. The crafty serpent focuses on this single limitation.

Disingenuously, then, the serpent begins by saying, "Did God say, 'You shall not eat from any tree in the garden?'" (v. 1b). Note the avoidance of any mention of all the positive possibilities otherwise open. There is simply a sweeping, though purposely vague, inquiry about prohibition. The woman responds rightly, pointing out the wide scope in which they have freedom, before mentioning the single prohibition and the divine warning about eating the fruit of that one tree lest they die (v. 3). The woman actually exaggerates the divine command: they are not even to "touch" the tree, whereas God had simply said not to eat of its fruit. The exaggeration suggests an element of fear: fear especially of death.[1] Fear, again, is something that the serpent can exploit. Already, at the risk of some anachronism, we are on "Ignatian territory," so to speak. The handling of freedom and the emotion of fear regarding the future are sensitive areas that the bad spirit is always prone to exploit.

The serpent's response, "You will not die" (v. 4), is not untrue. Although they eat the fruit of the tree, the couple in the end do not die. They are nonetheless rendered mortal; they will eventually die. More important, however, is the subtle way in which the serpent insinuates that the divine prohibition is self-serving on God's part: that God is trying to keep something from the human pair, keep them from sharing the godlike prerogative of knowing everything and so becoming "like God" in that sense, rather than like God in responsibility and love. In other words, the serpent is out to erode trust between God and the human pair God has created. Can they trust God if God has not told them everything, not given them absolutely everything? Once again, the serpent has placed the focus on the negative: what God appears *not* to have given, rather than on the abundance—including existence itself—that God has lavished on them.

The woman now (v. 6) notices that the fruit of the tree is good for food and beautiful to the eyes and "desirable for gaining wisdom." We might well ask, "What is wrong with gaining wisdom? Surely, that is a gift that God would want human beings to have." The problem is not the acquisition of wisdom but seeking to gain it in a way that bypasses God. Here, "wisdom" is not so much intellectual knowledge but skill in making decisions about life, discerning what is truly good and what is evil. If God is left out of that process, if human beings, who are creatures, use their freedom to act independently of their essential relationship with God, the result will not be good.

We see this result immediately within the story, as the woman takes the fruit, eats it, and gives it to her husband, who shares it with her (v. 6). What follows is a breakdown of intimacy and trust in all directions. Their "eyes are opened" to reveal their nakedness, which now becomes something shameful between them, so that they make loincloths out of fig leaves to hide it (v. 7). They hear the sound of God walking in the garden at the time of the evening breeze—a beautiful image of divine familiarity with the world of human beings and other creatures. But now, their hitherto "adult" relationship with God broken, they run from God like naughty children seeking to hide themselves from parental sight.

The breakdown of trust and intimacy in relationship is all the more striking in the divine "inquest" that follows (vv. 9–13). The man, who is questioned first, points to his nakedness and fear as excuses for seeking to hide from God. When questioned about eating the forbidden fruit, he blames the woman—the woman "that you [God] gave me," as though God should bear some of the blame as well (v. 12). When God turns to the woman, she in turn blames the serpent, who "tricked" her (v. 13). So there is blame all around.

With great dramatic effect, the divine pronouncement of judgment (vv. 14–19) proceeds in reverse order to the blaming, beginning with the serpent. The sentence pronounced on the serpent (vv. 14–15) has of course been interpreted in various ways—including a "messianic" sense, foreshadowing the theological understanding of Mary, Mother of Jesus, as the "new Eve." The original meaning, however, is more likely that of indicating the breakdown of harmonious relationship between human beings and the animal world, of which the serpent is here the representative. Meanwhile, the man and woman presumably sit back, thinking that their tactic of shifting the blame to the serpent has been successful, but God then turns to the woman (v. 16). From the originally equal companionship with the man, being wife and mother will involve pain; she will desire her husband but he will lord it over her. Although today we find this ancient explanation disturbing, let us at least note that the text, with surprising sensitivity, does recognize the painful and subordinate lot that woman has borne down the ages. It is something that was not part of God's original design but the result of failure on the human side. "This writer understood that patriarchy and related ills came as a consequence of sin, rather than being the divine intention."[2]

All the while, the man has been sitting back, satisfied that the blame rests on the serpent and the woman, leaving him free. That, however, is not the divine view. The man is equally responsible and must accept his own sanction—one that bears upon his relationship with the earth: his toil to produce food for his family will be laborious and burdensome, since the earth will not yield its produce easily (vv. 17–19).

The man is not cursed by God but the earth is: "Cursed is the ground because of you. In toil you shall eat of it all the days of your life" (v. 17c). As we shall see, Paul will take up a Jewish tradition drawn from this text and picture creation "groaning" to be set free from this curse, which it incurred, not of its own desire or fault, but because of the man's sin (Rom 8:19–22). This longing on the part of inanimate creation will be built into Paul's understanding of a "new creation" coming into being through God's intervention in Christ. In fact, Paul will see the whole of that intervention as designed to repair the breakdown of relationships in all directions— the intimacy between God and human beings, between human beings themselves, and at least in an extended sense, between humans and the remainder of creation. What Paul seems to have in mind, however, is not so much a restoration of something that prevailed originally and was then lost. In sending the Son into the world, God was not doing a "repair job" but rather bringing the original divine intent in Creation to fruition for the first time.

The reference to the man's having to labor until he returns to the dust from which he came (v. 19c) simply indicates the limit of his life. It does not suggest that death is a penalty for his sin, introduced as part of the sentence. Death is simply assumed. God will have another remedy for death.

In any case, human existence will go on because the pair will procreate. This seems to be implied in the otherwise somewhat intrusive note (v. 20) that the man named his wife "Eve, because she is the mother of all the living."

Meanwhile, God "adjusts" to the new situation brought about by the human lapse. The man and woman had already sought to clothe the nakedness they had come to regard as shameful; they attempted to remedy it with loincloths made of fig leaves sewn together (v. 7). Now God, who of course had not distanced himself from the pair because of their sin but "walked in the garden" and sought them out (v. 8), graciously provides much more effective clothing in the shape of animal skins (v. 21). But this divine adjustment to the situation does not mean that life can continue in the garden as before. There has to be an expulsion from the garden lest the human pair have access to the tree of life and so obtain the immortality that belongs to divine beings alone (vv. 22–24). Once again, we are in the realm of a symbolism that remains mysterious and elusive. "Likeness to God" does not mean ceasing to be creatures. In particular, it cannot include enjoying the immunity to death and decay that is the prerogative of divine being alone. That is why the human couple must not have access to the tree of life.

This is not, however, the end of the story. Our Christian faith presents the mission of the Son as an attempt to draw human beings, set free from sin and death, into the intimacy and trust intended by God from the start. Although physical mortality remains, such intimacy holds out the hope of sharing the divine eternal life. Not only Paul, in his reclaiming of the Genesis 1—3 traditions for Christ, but especially the Fourth Gospel and the First Letter of John, promote this view. Jesus says it memorably to Martha, the brother of Lazarus, whom he will shortly raise from the dead:

> I am the resurrection and the life. Those who believe in me, even though they die, will live, and everyone who lives and believes in me will never die. (John 11:25–26)

And in the First Letter of John, we are given the following assurance:

> See what love the Father has given us, that we should be called children of God; and that is what we are....Beloved, we are God's children now; what we will be has not yet been revealed. What we do know is this: when he is revealed, we will be like him, for we will see him as he is. (3:1–2)

REFLECTION

What emerges from all this? First, the sense that life is the gift of God, whose sole intent in our regard is to share existence with us. Second, this sharing of life, to be truly personal, necessarily involves freedom, intimacy, and trust. As such, it runs the risk of freedom being abused, trust eroded, and intimacy debased into immature defensiveness and blame. The story told in Genesis 3 does depict that sad development—in regard not only to the relationship between God and human beings, but also in regard to their mutual relationship, and the relations between themselves on the one hand and their wider environment on the other.

However, this breakdown is not the last word. God adjusts to failure on the human side and remains in relationship with human beings, albeit a relationship that is wounded and reduced. As the following chapters of Genesis show, faced with ever-increasing violence and sinfulness on the part of human beings, culminating in the wickedness that brings on the great flood, God does not abandon creation but continues to engage in dialogue and saving intervention (Genesis 6—9).

Such intervention culminates, of course, beyond all expectation in the incarnation and costly saving mission of the Son. When, according to Paul, believers, impelled by the Spirit, cry out "*Abba*, Father" (Rom 8:15; Gal 4:6–7), they are being taken up into the intimacy that exists between Father and Son, an intimacy that both restores the loss described in Genesis 3 and extends vastly beyond anything described or even imagined there. In due course, we will discuss at some length these passages and the intimacy to which they bear witness.

SUGGESTED SCRIPTURE

Genesis 3; Romans 1:18–23; Genesis 6—9; John 11:17–27; 1 John 3:1–2

PERSONAL REFLECTION

What image of God emerges for me from this sequence in Genesis 3?

Does this image of God challenge my "operative" image of God, that is, the view of God that underpins and shapes my living in a religious sense?

What factors in my life make for intimacy—with God, with fellow human beings?

What factors, on the contrary, lead me away from intimacy?

What results from this loss and what, with the help of God's grace, might be a remedy?

"HE EMPTIED HIMSELF..."
(PHIL 2:7)

We have been considering the vision of God as Creator and ourselves as creatures stemming from the two Creation accounts in Genesis 1—2. We also saw the way in which two celebrated hymnic passages in Colossians and Ephesians describe that divine project being realized in Christ. We then returned to Genesis and considered the human response to God as Creator set out in chapter 3, a response in which the original intimacy between God and human beings was ruptured by selfishness and mistrust on the human side.

Importantly, we have lingered on those early chapters of Genesis because so much of what is depicted there, especially in the figure of "the man" (Adam), is presupposed in Paul's portrayal of the interaction between human beings and God. Now, we return to Paul himself and treat of a passage in which the drama described in Genesis 1—3 runs very close to the surface. It is the well-known Christ-hymn from the second chapter of his Letter to the Philippians (2:6–11). It is one of the gems of the Pauline corpus of letters and has, rightly, found a place in the Liturgy of the Hours, being recited every Saturday at Evening Prayer.

Philippians is perhaps the most approachable of all Paul's letters. Certainly, it is the one where he pours out his spirituality most unreservedly. Paul is writing from prison. It was not customary in the Roman world to sentence offenders to a period of imprisonment. Prisons were for people awaiting trial and verdict. For those in prison, there were only two possible outcomes: release if you were found not guilty, execution if you were condemned. In the opening part of the letter, Paul reviews these two possibilities in his own case. Writing to what was perhaps his favorite community, one that as far as we know, had never given him any trouble, he does not hesitate to share his feelings about the two outcomes that lie before him:

> It is my eager expectation and hope that I will not be put to shame in any way, but that by my speaking with all boldness, Christ will be exalted now as always in my body, whether by life or by death. For me, to live is Christ and to die is gain. If I am to live in the flesh, that means fruitful labor for me; and I do not know which I prefer. I am hard pressed between the two: my desire is to depart and be with Christ, for that is far better; but to remain in the flesh is more necessary for you. (1:20–24)

Later he adds the following:

> Only, live your life in a manner worthy of the gospel of Christ, so that, whether I come and see you or am absent and hear about you, I will know that you are standing firm in one spirit, striving side by side with one mind for the faith of the gospel. (1:27)

Paul is writing what may in fact have been his last letter before execution in Rome. Despite this fateful context, the letter is full of exhortations to joy. He is urging this beloved community to live a life "worthy of the gospel" in all the various respects in which that worthiness is displayed. A key respect, of course, is unity and harmony in the community.

It is in the context of this specific concern that he introduces the Christ-hymn with the following exhortation:

> If then there is any encouragement in Christ, any
> consolation from love, any sharing in the Spirit, any
> compassion and sympathy, make my joy complete:
> be of the same mind, having the same love, being
> in full accord and of one mind. Do nothing from
> selfish ambition or conceit, but in humility regard
> others as better than yourselves. Let each of you
> look not to your own interests, but to the interests
> of others. Let the same mind be in you that was in
> Christ Jesus. (2:1–5)

There follows the Christ-hymn—a text already circulating,
it would seem, in the communities of believers before the
writing of Philippians, and therefore something familiar to
which Paul could appeal.

Before considering the hymn itself, let us consider briefly
those characteristic Pauline words at the start: "If there is any
encouragement [*paraklēsis*] in Christ…." In some respects,
"encouragement" sums up everything Paul is trying to give his
communities and get them to give to each other. A tiny
minority living in a largely hostile world, they need encouragement more than anything else. Then the remaining terms
and phrases: "any consolation [deriving from] love"; any
"compassion" (*splagchna*, literally, fellow feeling coming from
the depths of one's heart); any "sympathy" (*oiktirmoi*). If these
qualities prevail, Paul's joy will be complete. He then warns
them about the opposite attitude:

> Do nothing from selfish ambition or conceit, but
> in humility regard others as better than yourselves.
> Let each of you look not to your own interests, but
> to the interests of others. (vv. 3–4)

For Paul, the key to unity in a community is that people
act unselfishly: selfishness is the polar opposite of love. It

is to drive this point home that he introduces the Christ-hymn, which is all about the unselfishness of Christ, with the exhortation: "Let the same mind be in you that was in Christ Jesus" (v. 5). Here, "mind" refers not just to intellectual understanding but to attitude, to the "mind-set" that leads to a determined form of action.

THE CHRIST-HYMN (PHIL 2:6–11)

The hymn proper (vv. 6–11) then follows in three stanzas, each stating the "mind" of Christ in the three stages of what may be called his "career": his pretemporal existence with God before the incarnation; his human life up to death on the cross; his exaltation as "Lord" following his resurrection from the dead. In each of these stages, as we shall see, he displays the self-emptying attitude that is the essence of love for Paul, and indeed the essence of divine love as revealed in every way by Christ.

Let us consider the first stanza:

Who, though he was in the form of God,
did not regard equality with God
as something to be exploited for selfish gain,
but emptied himself,
taking the form of a slave,
being born in human likeness. (vv. 6–7)

Essentially, this stanza describes the Incarnation: the "entrance" of the Son into the human world from a "before" with God. Hovering behind the lines is the first account of Creation in Genesis that we have already considered, where human beings are said to be created "in the image and likeness of God," and in view of that, given dominion—or lordship—over all the other living creatures on the face of the earth

"He emptied himself…"

(Gen 1:26–28). The hymn sees the preexistent Christ as not simply "like God" in the way of all human beings but having a likeness to God that amounts to "equality with God." This very early Christian document—composed perhaps only twenty years after Christ's all too human death on the cross—is attributing to him, in a pretemporal mode of existence, a unique divine status.

The next line is very important. For Christ, being "like God" in this unique sense was not something to be exploited for selfish gain. The underlying rare Greek word here, *harpagmon*, refers to something snatched or grabbed for one's own benefit without regard for the needs of others—as, for example, when, coming upon a purse or pocketbook on the sidewalk, one simply appropriates its contents for oneself. Contrary to such self-serving behavior, being "like God" in the exalted sense of "equality with God" means self-emptying. Here, the hymn is virtually giving a "definition" of God in terms of self-emptying love.

Being "like God" in this radical way impels the Son to enter human existence to effect a rescue mission for creation. Why is a rescue mission necessary? Because humanity, created by God for lordship of the universe in an unselfish, nonexploitative way, has forfeited that dignity and, from being godlike, has fallen into a "slave-like" existence. That is why the hymn talks of Christ, who was "in the form of God," taking on the "form of a slave."

Slavery was a pervasive social phenomenon in the ancient world. Perhaps 40 percent of the population of the Roman Empire were in some form of slavery, and many members of the communities of believers, if not slaves themselves, belonged to families of slaves who had been freed. A key contrast in social terms was that between master or "lord," on the one hand, and slave, on the other. So slavery was a powerful image for the hymn to evoke. For Christ, who was uniquely "in the form" of God and "lord" on that account, to take on "the form of a slave," meant total self-emptying. Yet it was precisely his likeness to God that led him to such a move, since the essence of God is love.

In what sense does the hymn think of human existence as "slavery"? This may seem to strike a very pessimistic note, but it is integral to Paul's understanding. What human beings are enslaved to is a pattern of selfishness that, in his view, is the root or cause of all sin. That pattern can only be broken by being overwhelmed and conquered by utterly unselfish love. Hence, the mission of the Son in the world: to be the incarnation of divine love, strong enough—more than strong enough—to break the grip of sin.

The second stanza of the hymn describes this mission of the Son very briefly:

> And being found in human form,
> he humbled himself
> and became obedient to the point of death—
> even death on a cross. (vv. 7d–8)

"Being found" is just biblical idiom for "being"; it doesn't have the sense of being "found" after being lost. The hymn at this point (v. 8) goes on to state that, not only did the Son undergo the self-emptying involved in incarnation; the same self-emptying pattern continued in his human life as he became obedient to the point of death, even death on a cross. Death by crucifixion was, of course, the form of execution reserved for slaves and rebels against the Roman state. Slaves had no choice as to whether they would be obedient; they had to carry out the tasks assigned by their masters or "look out"!

In what sense, though, was Christ in his human life "obedient unto death." Clearly, he was not obedient to Death, as though Death were some kind of master. Nor, I believe, is there any question of his being obedient to a command to die

40

imposed by the Father. Rather, his obedience consisted in the fact that his entire life represented obedience to who he was as the Father's Son, the incarnation of divine, self-emptying love. This "obedience" of love, of truth to who he was, inevitably brought him into conflict with those in seats of power in his society who resented the company he kept, the teaching he gave, and the prophetic denunciations he uttered against those who oppressed and laid burdens on the poor— the particular objects of his Father's love and care. In his society, a collision between the values he espoused and the interests of those in power was inevitable—as it would also be nearly two millennia later for Archbishop Oscar Romero in El Salvador.

As mentioned earlier, allusion to the Creation story hovers in the background to this hymn. In this depiction of Christ as "obedient unto death," it is almost certain that we are meant to find a contrast to one who was "disobedient" in regard to God, namely, Adam.

Here, we see Paul's understanding of Christ replaying successfully the role that Adam muffed. In the words of Cardinal Newman's own Christ-hymn, "Praise to the Holiest in the Height":

> O wisest love that flesh and blood,
> That did in Adam fail,
> Should strive afresh against the foe,
> should strive and should prevail.

And more recently by Archbishop Rowan Williams:

> Arguably what is going on in the work of redemption is, as St. Irenaeus first put it, the reversal of Adam's mistake. Adam's resentment at not being God is transfigured by Christ into the free acceptance of not being God. That's what Philippians 2 is all about.[3]

Christ's obedience, then, consisted in his living out a human life that in every way gave expression to the divine, self-emptying love—and did so to the point where that love brought him inexorably to the cross.

The third stanza of the hymn (vv. 9–11) portrays Christ in his postresurrection life. It doesn't actually speak of resurrection from the dead; that is presupposed. It speaks rather of his exaltation by the Father and "installation" as Lord (*kyrios*) of the universe.

> Therefore God also highly exalted him
> and gave him the name that is above every name,
> so that at the name of Jesus
> every knee should bend,
> in heaven and on earth and under the earth,
> and every tongue should confess
> that Jesus Christ is Lord [*kyrios*],
> to the glory of God the Father. (vv. 9–11)

Here, again, the parallel/contrast with the first account of Creation hovers in the background. There, as we noted, God created human beings in the divine image and likeness and gave them "lordship" over creation, to be in effect "viceroys" of God in the universe. Human sinfulness, however, abused that lordship and reduced the human situation to its polar opposite: slavery. Through entry into that situation and through his obedient love within it unto death, Christ has reclaimed for human beings the lordship, not just of animate creation, but of the entire universe. To make this final point, the hymn quotes from Isaiah:

> Turn to me and be saved, all the ends of the earth!
> For I am God, and there is no other. By myself
> I have sworn, from my mouth has gone forth in
> righteousness a word that shall not return: "To me

every knee shall bow, every tongue shall swear."
(Isa 45:22–23)

What is remarkable is that the homage of all creation, which the Isaiah text claims will be given to God alone (*For I am God, and there is no other*) is now attributed directly to Christ.

This is why "the name" that the text speaks of being bestowed by God upon Christ is not his proper name, *Jesus*, but rather his titular name, *Lord* (*kyrios*). The meaning is that, whenever the name *Jesus* is mentioned, all creation immediately thinks *Lord*—just as whenever the name *Barack Obama* is mentioned, everyone thinks *President of the United States*—and in view of that title, the whole of creation responds in homage. Or, in other words, the homage of the universe that the Isaiah text attributed to God ("the Lord" [*kyrios*]) is now to be given to the risen Christ because God has conferred the divine name and lordship upon him.

We should not, however, neglect to note the final phrase: "Jesus Christ is 'Lord,' *to the glory of God the Father*" (v. 11c). In this final stanza, we find the same note of self-emptying love prevalent in the first two. As raised and exalted, and as bearing before the universe the name of God (*kyrios*), Jesus is no rival to the Father. On the contrary, his lordship is directed not to his own glory but to that of the Father. In effect, he is wholly the instrument of bringing the universe into the submission to God that was proclaimed in Isaiah 45.

Of course, as we are all too aware from our day-to-day experience of the world, this role of Christ is not something accomplished but a work in progress. The Christ-hymn quoted by Paul, in the way of liturgical texts, takes us to the final state of affairs, to what is still for us a matter of hope. Christ must continue, as risen Lord, his messianic mission until the end of time. Paul spells this out more conformably to the actual situation in 1 Corinthians 15:

For he must reign until he has put all his enemies under his feet. The last enemy to be destroyed is death. For "God has put all things in subjection under his feet." But when it says, "All things are put in subjection," it is plain that this does not include the one who put all things in subjection under him. When all things are subjected to him, then the Son himself will also be subjected to the one who put all things in subjection under him, so that God may be all in all. (1 Cor 15:25–28)

Here, there is the sense of an ongoing messianic mission, rather than one accomplished once and for all. However, what is said in verse 28 is totally at one with the final stanza of the Christ-hymn in Philippians: the "subjection" of the universe to the Son is directed totally to the glory of God.

REFLECTION

I have discussed this Pauline hymn in considerable detail because it so effectively communicates Paul's overall vision in which the Creator's original design for human beings within the universe, a design continually frustrated by human sinfulness, is being realized at last through the messianic mission of Christ. At the heart of it is the sense of human beings created in the image and likeness of God. If the essence of the Godhead is love, then to be created in the divine likeness should mean to be set on the path of reflecting that likeness in self-sacrificial love. Only through such love can the world be truly humanized in realization of the divine design. When human beings languished in alienation from God, helplessly far from that realization, Christ entered into the human situation of "slavery," at great cost, the cost of love, to redeem us from slavery and restore the possibility of love.

"He emptied himself…"

Today, contemplate the crucifix and ask the Lord for the grace to see it as the revelation of love, the costly rescue of us and our world from all that is opposed to love and is destructive of true humanity on that account.

SUGGESTED SCRIPTURE

Philippians 1:18–27; 2:1–11; 2:12–18; Isaiah 45:22–23; Jeremiah 20:7–12

PERSONAL REFLECTION

Before the crucifix, and in the light of the Christ-hymn, one might put to oneself, as Ignatius recommends (*Spiritual Exercises*, §53), the following three questions:

What have I done for Christ?
What am I doing for Christ?
What ought I do for Christ?

DAY 3

⚬◦❦◦⚬

THE MYSTERY OF SIN

So far, we have spent much of the retreat considering the opening chapters of Genesis. This is appropriate because, in so much of what Paul writes, he presupposes the vision of God and God's designs for human beings emerging from these chapters. The central understanding of God that emerges is that of one who simply wants to share life with human beings as abundantly and richly as human freedom will allow. Freedom is necessary if that sharing is to be truly personal, but freedom, on the human side, runs the risk that it will be abused or end up victim to the false sowing of mistrust that will poison or severely limit human relationship with God. This is the outcome depicted in the story told in Genesis 3. In its highly mythological way, it is not a story about "back there"—although, to some extent, that is how Paul read it. It is a perennially valid account of how human beings fail in relating to God and of the consequences of that failure for relationships in all directions.

Of course, this is to state only the negative. Against it, surrounding it, and ultimately eclipsing the record of failure, the Bible sets the constant divine "adjustment" to the situation, the "grace" story that precedes, accompanies, and ultimately overcomes the "sin" story—a victory of divine grace that will culminate in the death and resurrection of Jesus Christ.

This biblical sense of two "stories"—a "sin" story and a (yet more powerful) "grace" story—abroad in the world and encompassing each and every human life is one that Paul wholeheartedly embraced and that Ignatius, in his own way, also discovered and put into practical effect. Such an understanding of human life, while central to the *Spiritual Exercises* as a whole, appears most explicitly in the "Rules for Discernment," appended in two sets toward the end (§§313–27, 328–33). Like Paul, Ignatius came to believe that each human life was lived out under the "tug" of two opposing forces. God's grace is constantly trying to draw us more fully into the "grace" story, with its outcome of sharing the divine eternal life—and its beneficent effect on other human beings and the environment as a whole. Against this, each human life is influenced by the opposing "sin" story, with precisely the opposite effects. We do not live out our lives on neutral terrain or "no man's land." Without being overly dualistic, we can say that we are engaged in a battle, or rather, conflicting forces are fighting over us, to win us either for freedom and life, or captivity and death. In the view of both Paul and Ignatius—and, judging also from the serpent's behavior—in the view of the original account in Genesis 3, the greatest weapon on the negative side is the element of deception, of concealment, the temptation through the appearance of good.[1]

Within this overall perspective, let us now consider Paul's idea of "sin"—never losing sight, however, of the equally Pauline conviction about the prevailing power of grace. As he says at one point, "Where sin abounded, grace 'super-abounded'" (Rom 5:20b).

THE ESSENCE OF "SIN"

Paul has a very sophisticated understanding of sin. He is not much interested in "sins"—the actual instances of sinning, such as murder, adultery, lying, stealing, and so on. These for him are only the symptoms, the outward manifestations of a much more deep-seated "virus" that is his principal concern. The Greek word for sin—*hamartia*—appears over sixty times in Paul's letters. Predominantly, and especially in the Letter to the Romans, it appears in the singular, not the plural. Paul speaks overwhelmingly of sin as a mysterious negative force within human lives, ranged against the positive influence of divine grace.

Rather than a specific offence against God—although Paul does, of course, presuppose such an understanding of concrete instances of sin—in the central chapters of Romans, notably chapters 5—8, Paul personifies sin for rhetorical effect, portraying it as a tyrant power or slave-master that has human beings in its grip. For Paul, rather than something to be punished or forgiven—though again he presupposes that traditional understanding (see Rom 3:21–26)—sin is a captivity or enslavement from which human beings need to be set free. That is why he speaks about the saving work of Christ as a "redemption," employing the word (*apolytrōsis*) used to describe the liberation of those who have been taken captive in war and, as was customary at the time, sold into a situation of slavery. Their relatives and friends could only secure their freedom by paying a price. "Redemption," then, has the sense of freedom—but at a cost, a cost that Paul sees to have been paid by Christ.

What, then, is the essence of this "captivity" or "enslavement" that Paul sees as "sin"? For Paul, sin denotes a radical selfishness that poisons relationships in all directions: to God, to one's fellow human beings, to one's body, and to the wider, non-human world (Rom 8:19–21). Sin is the tendency to refer all things to my own advantage, to adopt an "exploitative" attitude to everything outside myself, rather than the "contemplative" attitude that allows each and everything outside myself to have its own autonomy. For a concise summary, we cannot do better than a phrase, ultimately derived from St. Augustine, describing sin—or, more accurately, the sinful human being—as *homo incurvatus in se* (literally, "man turned in on himself"). As you will appreciate, this is the exact opposite of the Pauline sense of the divine outreach in love manifested by the "self-emptying" disposition of Christ (Phil 2:6–8; also see Rom 15:3).

In Paul's view, sin in this fundamental sense forms a carapace or crust around a person, a false self, offering a deluded security destructive of relationship. Encased in this false self, a person tends to define him- or herself against others in an attempt thereby to bolster one's identity and self-worth. (A classic biblical example is provided by the Pharisee in Luke's parable of the Pharisee and the tax collector [18:9–14]. He enhances the recital of his virtues through a comparison with the tax collector conveniently at hand down the back.) In the specific context in which Paul wrote, especially in Galatians and Romans, the feature that particularly fed this false self or provided opportunity for sin to do so was confidence ("boasting") in possession and observance of the Mosaic Law. There was nothing wrong with the Law in itself. But granted the human tendency to turn all things to one's own advantage, the Law provided a fertile field for sin to take hold in this way. The Law was so intimately bound up with Jewish identity that it fostered and reinforced negative social divisions that could build up the false sense of special status to the detriment of the new reality of graced community that God was bringing about in Christ. Coming to faith in Christ and acting out that commitment socially and ecclesially in the sacrament of baptism means "putting to death" this false self and the attitudes that foster it.

Thus, Paul recalls in Galatians (2:11–15) a vigorous rebuke he gave to Peter ("Cephas") at Antioch. In that community made up of believers of both Jewish and non-Jewish (Gentile) origin, Peter had initially shared table-fellowship with all regardless of ethnic origin. Later, under pressure from a more Law-observant party associated with James, he withdrew himself from table fellowship with Gentiles. In Paul's eyes, this flew directly in the face of the gospel. Speaking as a representative of believers of Jewish origin, Peter included, he protests,

> For through the law I died to the law, so that I might live to God. I have been crucified with Christ; and it is no longer I who live, but it is Christ who lives in me. And the life I now live in the flesh I live by faith in the Son of God, who loved me and gave himself for me. (Gal 2:19–20)

The "I" who "died to the law" in being "crucified with Christ," the "I" that "no longer lives," is the false "I" that, on the basis of adherence to the Law, built up its identity through relegating believers of non-Jewish background to inferior status. Later in the letter, Paul formulates the same idea in broader categories:

> As many of you as were baptized into Christ have clothed yourselves with Christ. There is no longer Jew or Greek, slave or free, male and female; for all of you are one person in Christ Jesus. (Gal 3:27–28)

Of course, Paul doesn't mean that these divisions—ethnic, social, gender—have been entirely abolished. His point is that, as far as relationships within the believing community are concerned, they should not count. If they do, they reflect a divisive attempt to build up one's own identity at the expense of others. This flies directly in the face of what God has done in the costly death of Christ (2:21).

Note that in the earlier Galatians passage, Paul said, "It is no longer I who live"; in so far as "I" live, "I live by faith in the Son of God, who loved me and delivered himself up for me." There is perhaps something deeply mystical here: the "death" of the old ego and the creation of a new, true "I" that is being brought to life by the experience of being loved by Christ. There is nothing so fruitful for growth in human beings as being loved by others: we are loved into life. Paul has this very strong sense of the new "I" being loved into new life by the Son of God. It is surely very consoling for us believers of a later time that this most personal expression in the New Testament of being loved by Jesus comes not from Peter or John or from other disciples who walked with him in Palestine but from one who never "knew him according to the flesh" (2 Cor 5:16), one who only came to know him, in fleeting glimpse, as risen Lord (1 Cor 9:1; 15:8; Gal 1:16).

To sum up, we can say that sin for Paul is simply the opposite of divine love. It is fundamentally the refusal to engage in the trusting and loving relationship with God that God is holding out to human beings on the basis that God is God and we are creatures, albeit ones called to share most intimately in the divine communion of love that is the Trinity. Paul may not have a formulated theology of the Trinity such as the Christian tradition arrived at in subsequent centuries. But it is remarkable how often his expressions take on a "trinitarian cast." The most notable instance, familiar to us from the greeting that begins the eucharistic celebration, is the farewell blessing at the end of 2 Corinthians:

> The grace of our Lord Jesus Christ, the love of God
> [the Father] and the communion of the Holy Spirit
> be with you all. (13:13)

If we probe all those terms—"grace," "love," "communion"—this surely expresses Paul's understanding of Christian life as lived in the embracing outreach of the divine life to us. Sin is the self-absorbed, untrusting turning away from that outreach of love.

THE FATAL ENCOUNTER WITH "SIN" (ROM 7:7–13)

To complete the picture in regard to sin, let us consider Paul's "take" on the Genesis 3 story as set out briefly in Romans 7:7–13. Curiously, he casts sin in the role of the serpent:

> What, then, shall we say? That the law is sin? God forbid! But I would not have known sin except through the law. For I would not have known covetousness, if the law had not said, *"You must not covet."* But sin, seizing its opportunity, by means of the commandment worked in me all manner of covetousness. For apart from the law sin is dead. I was alive once, apart from the law. But when the commandment came, sin sprang to life. I died and the commandment, which was meant to lead to life, turned out to be death for me. For sin, seizing its opportunity, by means of the commandment deceived me and through it killed me. (Rom 7:7–11)

It is commonly, though not universally, agreed that the "I" who speaks here is not Paul speaking personally about his own experience in an autobiographical way. Rather, concerned at this point in Romans to stress the impotence of the Law to address the problem of sin, Paul projects that impotence on the situation described in Genesis 3. He identifies the situation of those confronted by the Law (principally Jews, but also, if some early Christian teachers had their way, converts from the Gentile world) with that of Adam. Adam was also faced with "law," albeit in the shape of a single prohibition (not to eat the fruit of the tree of the knowledge of good and evil). Paul brings together the situation of Adam and that of the Israelites confronted by the Mosaic Law at Mount Sinai by reducing the entire Law to a single prohibition against "coveting": *You must not covet* (v. 7). Of course, "coveting" was involved only in the case of one (or, in the Catholic reckoning, two) of the Ten Commandments (of one's neighbor's wife and one's neighbor's goods [Exod 20:17]) but Paul, likely drawing on a Jewish tradition, sees "coveting" as the font of all sin, as lying behind all concrete sinful activity. *Covet* translates a Greek verb (*epithymeō*) cognate with a noun expressing "desire" (*epithymia*), so that the prohibition against coveting can also be understood as forbidding desire. When we remember the statement in Genesis 3 to the effect that the one tree forbidden to the couple was seen by the woman as "desirable" (Gen 3:6), we can see the connection that Paul was making between the situation of Adam and that of the Israelites confronted with the Law (specifically with the Commandments): what both were facing was a prohibition against the "coveting/desiring" that, in Paul's view, lies at the heart of all sin.

Desire (*epithymia*) almost always has a negative connotation in Paul's writings. He seems to understand desire as the aspiration for the complete moral autonomy that belongs to God alone, the autonomy symbolized by the tree of the knowledge of good and evil. As the "I" explains in Romans 7:7–11, it was the prohibition, along with some deceptive advice from the serpent ("sin"), that provoked the "desire" for such autonomy, the very thing that the commandment sought to exclude. Satisfying "desire" in this sense involves regarding all other creatures, and indeed the relationship with God, as exploitable for one's own self-interest alone. To act on it leads, in Paul's view, to death, whereas, in itself, the commandment was meant to preserve the first couple from death and lead to life (v. 10b).

In retrieving the story of Adam in this way, Paul is, of course, analyzing the human situation apart from the grace of Christ. He would not deny that deep in the human heart there are good desires, fostered by grace: above all the most radical desire for God, of which St. Augustine spoke so eloquently and famously at the beginning of the *Confessions*: "You have made us for yourself, O Lord, and our hearts are restless until they rest in you" (1:1). But what Paul is attempting to show (in a very Ignatian way, I anachronistically believe) is how "sin," playing now the role of the serpent, acts deceptively to employ a good thing—the commandment that was meant to be protective of life—for a destructive purpose. The Adamic "I" tells a story true of every human being confronted simply by moral demand aside from the healing effects of grace. As Ignatius explains in the first set of his "Rules for the Discernment of Spirits" (*Exercises*, §315), for those who are proceeding from good to better, the bad spirit does not tempt them to overtly repugnant bad behavior. The bad spirit acts more craftily and deceptively by tempting people through the appearance of good. The mother or father of a family, with weighty responsibilities, might be tempted to leave them and take up a call to become a missionary or an aid worker ministering to some desperate human situation overseas. The sacrifice involved might be heroic, but it would be a case of what appears to be the best becoming the enemy of the good—and right. The sheer heroism, while good in itself, could be something that subtly plays on one's "desire" in the bad sense, one's aspiration to build up the false self that gets in the way of true relationship with God and others. Playing the deceptive role of the serpent in the Garden, "sin" can exploit such situations, masking from us our real motivations and sowing distrust and confusion in our relationship to God.

REFLECTION

As noted earlier, Paul presents "sin" primarily as a plight, a captivity from which one needs to be set free. It is a radical enslavement to a selfish, exploitative pattern of behavior that is the very antithesis of the divine outpouring of self-emptying love. Paul does have a sense of sin in a more traditional mode as an offence against God requiring forgiveness, achieved through the atoning work of Jesus Christ (Rom 3:24–25; 2 Cor 5:18–21). However, that is not the main thrust of his understanding. God's readiness to forgive is presupposed; the divine initiative is never in doubt. For Paul, especially as apparent in Romans, sin is a captivity to radical selfishiness that sets up a pattern of selfish behavior (sinful acts) from which human beings cannot by their own efforts break free—despite, in many cases, an ardent desire to do so (see especially Rom 7:14–25). It is akin in this way to an addiction—as to substance abuse, alcoholism, pornography, gambling, and so on. The remedy for Paul is not the imposition of the Law, well-intentioned though that may be and even necessary at an early stage. The remedy is the liberating power of the Spirit (Rom 8:2), unleashed through the death and resurrection of Jesus, as the felt experience of divine love. That alone can ensure that, where sin has abounded, grace will "super-abound" (see Rom 5:20b).

This idea of the prevailing power of grace over sin is what prevents Paul's spirituality from being pessimistic, although some passages in his letters taken in isolation from the wider context (as unfortunately tends to happen in the Lectionary used at Mass) can give that impression. It is never right to consider Paul's profound exploration of sin apart from his equally profound expression of the power of God's grace. It is no accident, then, that the section of Romans where he most deeply explores the mystery of sin (chapters 5—8) has as its overriding theme the hope that springs from God's love (Rom 5:5; 8:31–39).

SUGGESTED SCRIPTURE

Psalms 50 (51); 102 (103); 142 (143); Luke 15:1–32 (parables of the lost); 18:9–14 (parable of the Pharisee and the tax collector)

PERSONAL REFLECTION

Always conscious of being in the presence of God as a God of grace and acceptance, ask yourself:

Does Paul's profound sense of sin as "captivity" to (addictive) self-seeking have any resonance in my life?
Can I detect any ways in which the bad spirit may be tempting me under the appearance of good?

RECONCILIATION

We have been reflecting on Paul's view of the mystery of "sin." While this may have been a fairly negative exercise, keep in mind that Paul only thinks of sin in the context of the superior and overwhelming power of grace, of God's unmerited love. Like all the great figures of the Christian tradition who have experienced a profound conversion—St. Augustine, Martin Luther, St. Ignatius of Loyola, John Wesley, John Bunyan, to name some of the most prominent—Paul can plumb the depths of sin and alienation from God precisely because he has an even greater sense of being held by grace. We have to keep this in mind when we are tempted to think that his theology moves along lines that are overly pessimistic.

RECONCILING THE WORLD (2 COR 5:13—6:2)

Now, to my mind, the text that best sums up Paul's grasp of what God was doing through Christ to counter human alienation and reclaim the world for the original purpose of creation is 2 Cor 5:13—6:2. It occurs in a context where Paul is reminding the Corinthians, currently disaffected from him, of the true nature of his mission.

Speaking in the plural ("we") to include the coworkers —Timothy and Silvanus (see 2 Cor 1:19)—who are his companions in the mission, Paul begins:

> For if we are beside ourselves, it is for God; if we are in our right mind, it is for you. (2 Cor 5:13)

"Being beside ourselves" (v. 13) seems to refer to ecstatic experiences of some kind, such as speaking in tongues, or even the mystical transports mentioned later in the letter (12:1–4). Paul did not discount the value of such religious experiences (see 1 Cor 14:18–19). However, in the face of the Corinthians' apparently prizing them above all other gifts of the Spirit, he tended to relativize their value, ranking them simply as one class among several gifts of the Spirit—and not the most useful at that. So being "in one's right mind" was just as important for an apostle as being able to turn on displays of ecstasy. In fact, it was more useful in apostolic ministry: hence "If we are in our right mind, it is for you."

Then in a beautiful formulation, Paul turns to the real motivation of his mission:

> For the love of Christ urges us on, because we are convinced that one has died for all; therefore all have died. And he died for all, so that those who live might live no longer for themselves, but for him who died and was raised for them (vv. 14–15).

The phrase "urges us on" translates the Greek verb *synechein*, which is open to at least three distinct meanings. First, "hold together"—as when you're holding a number of parcels in your arms and trying to get into your car without dropping any of them. The sense of the love of Christ—that is, Christ's love for us—holding the believing community together in love is attractive and certainly true. It introduces an idea somewhat foreign to the *immediate* context, however. A second meaning would be that of "enclose"—as, for example, by a fence or surrounding stockade. Not so attractive and, again, not relevant to the context. The third meaning is more subtle and can be interpreted in a variety of ways: "press in on," "constrain," "control," or "urge on." The last interpretation, "urge on," could be linked to the other three in that by putting pressure on someone from all sides, you compel them to move.

A little more shaky on linguistic grounds but very attractive is the translation in the *Jerusalem Bible*: "For the love of Christ overwhelms us." Paul, who for a time persecuted the early believers—and in them persecuted Christ (Acts 9:4–5)—has a strong conviction of Christ's personal love. As he says in the text from Galatians that we have already considered, "I live now by faith in the Son of God, who loved me and delivered himself up for me" (2:20). It is easy to understand him saying to fellow believers, "The love of Christ overwhelms us"—not in the sense of constraining our freedom but by so catching us up in the rhythm of his unselfish love as to free us from all less worthy attachments.

Here (2 Cor 5:14), Paul is extending that very personal sense of Christ's love to the entire community of believers. The love of Christ, who died for us (literally, "for all") should be simply the overwhelming consideration that captures us and guides our entire life and action. That Christ "has died for all" means that all who attach themselves to him, through faith and baptism, have also "died" with him, that is, died to sin and any claims made against them because of sin (Rom 6:3–4, 6, 11). They (we) simply cannot live in a way determined by the "slavery to sin," the radical "being turned in on self," that characterized the old situation. On the contrary, they should "live no longer for themselves, but for him who died and was raised for them" (see also Rom 14:7–9). That is, they should live with the self-sacrificial love that Christ displayed in his earthly life and that now, as risen Lord, he continues to live out in the bodily life of believers, those who live "in him" (Rom 6:12–13). The Corinthians should understand that it is this unselfish love of Christ that is the driving force of Paul's mission.

In the following two verses, Paul contrasts, as he very

often tends to do, the old situation—the negative—with the new—the positive:

> From now on, therefore, we regard no one from a human point of view; even though we once knew Christ from a human point of view, we know him no longer in that way. So if anyone is in Christ, there is a new creation: everything old has passed away; see, everything has become new! (vv. 16–17)

Regarding anyone "from a human point of view" means regarding them—and assessing their worth—in terms of the categories prevalent in the old order ("Jew"/"Greek," "slave"/"free," "male"/ "female" [see Gal 3:28]), the categories that have been rendered unimportant, transcended in the life in Christ. Something so fundamental has changed that the old ways of seeing and understanding—and, more profoundly, of evaluating—must be replaced with a new way of seeing and understanding.[2]

The added remark about no longer "knowing Christ in that way" is possibly a sideswipe on Paul's part at those rival teachers who put him down on the basis that, unlike Peter, John, and the original disciples who walked with Jesus during his pre-passion life, Paul was a "Johnny-come-lately" as far as discipleship was concerned, and therefore, of inferior status—and possibly not to be recognized as a true apostle.

All this, however, has been swept aside by the new era— the "new creation"—that has dawned for those "in Christ," that is, those who have been joined to the risen Lord through faith and baptism (see also Gal 6:15). By saying, "everything old has passed away; see, everything has become new!" Paul is once again echoing Isaiah:

> Do not remember the former things,
> or consider the things of old.
> I am about to do a new thing. (43:18–19)

For Paul—as for all the New Testament writers—Isaiah is the prophet who most notably indicated the salvation that God would bring about in the Messianic Age. It is nothing less than a "new creation" or, rather, a realization for the first time of the design that God intended for creation from the beginning.

Hovering in the background, behind this "creation" language, is Paul's sense of Christ as the new "Adam," the ancestor or prototype of humanity renewed in the image of God. One enters into this lineage by being baptized "into" Christ. (Paul always speaks in this dynamic way of baptism: one is baptized "into" Christ, not just "in Christ.") Through baptism, one enters into Christ's death, the death he died for all, to overcome through his loving obedience the entire burden of human sin to set us free from death—not in the sense that we shall not die physically, but in the sense that physical death will not mean eternal death but, on the contrary, full entrance into the risen life of Christ.

At verse 18, Paul records his understanding of the apostolic mission on which he is engaged. He places it firmly within the great sweep of God's redemptive action for the world in Christ. As previously noted, it is perhaps the Apostle's most complete statement of this divine movement in our regard:

> All this is from God, who reconciled us to himself through Christ, and has given us the ministry of reconciliation; that is, in Christ God was reconciling the world to himself, not counting their trespasses against them, and entrusting the message of reconciliation to us. So we are ambassadors for Christ, since God is making his appeal through us; we entreat you on behalf of Christ, be reconciled to God. (vv. 18–20)

As is immediately obvious, central to this extended statement is the language and image of "reconciliation."

We can think of reconciliation operating in two rather different ways. In the first scenario, two parties who have been at war or at least hostile to each other for a long time eventually, and more or less independently, decide that enough is enough. They are ready, usually with the aid of a mediator, to make peace rather than war. This is what occurred, albeit imperfectly, in the lead up to the Good Friday agreement between Catholic and Protestant communities in Northern Ireland. In the second scenario, one of the hostile parties eventually wants reconciliation while the other remains hostile. The first party then takes the risk of reaching out in the face of the hostility and offering peace—a costly exercise if the offer is rebuffed. President Obama, when he first came to office, offered something akin to this one-sided proposal of reconciliation to countries hostile to the United States such as Iran, referring to it as "the outstretched hand."

It is reconciliation of this latter kind that Paul sees to be operative on a divine scale in this passage. God has reached out to an alienated world and, in the person of the Son acting as representative (New Adam) of the entire race, brought about radical reconciliation. God has paid the cost of that reconciliation in the passion and death of Jesus. The gospel that Paul proclaims is a summons to human beings to align themselves through faith with that reconciliation freely offered by God and so enter the new creation.

In this regard, of course, we have to come to terms with the negative presupposition on Paul's part, namely, that, aside from Christ, the world is radically alienated from God. In the Western theological tradition, influenced especially by St. Augustine, the alienation has found traditional formulation in the doctrine of "original sin," a doctrine that has had a hard time over recent decades and which is sorely in need of a satisfactory reformulation beyond that stated centuries ago by the Council of Trent, which the *Catechism of the Catholic Church* (§§396–409) simply restates. Paul doesn't really explain how human beings got into this state of alienation. To some extent, he attributes it to Adam—an explanation that we can hardly find satisfactory on the basis of a modern scientific understanding of human origins. To some extent, however, he posits a universal human ratification of this "original" Adamic sin (Rom 5:12d: "inasmuch as all sinned").[3] We shall consider this problematic text in greater depth later on. For the present, setting aside the question as to how human beings got into the state of alienation from God, let us simply note Paul's presupposition that all human lives stand in need of being touched by the healing grace of Christ and the reconciliation with God that he brings. In Christ, God is freely offering this reconciliation to the world, "not counting," as Paul says, "their trespasses against them" (v. 19).

Paul's own role in this project is that of being "ambassador for Christ" (v. 20). The understanding of ambassador here would not be that of the more usual scenario where hitherto hostile nations might choose to exchange ambassadors following the making of peace. Operative, rather, would be the much more dangerous undertaking of being emissaries sent into hostile territory to make the offer of peace—very much exposed to the risk of rebuff and retaliation.

Because this offer of reconciliation is the heart of the gospel, offered to those not yet personally reconciled with God, it is at first sight somewhat strange that Paul adds the following: "We entreat you on behalf of Christ, be reconciled to God" (v. 20b). It is strange because in this letter, as in all his letters, he is writing to people who are already believers, hence already reconciled to God through faith and baptism "into Christ." In the immediate context of the letter, however, Paul's call for reconciliation is not anomalous. There have been difficulties in his relationship with the community in Corinth, many of whose members have shown preference for other teachers who have come to the city after his departure. Paul is asking the Corinthians, then, to reconcile with himself. His point is that reconciliation with God is not a once-off thing; it must be continually lived out and continually passed on. (This is exactly the point made so much more dramatically in Jesus' parable of the unforgiving servant [Matt 18:23–35]: having received an immense cancellation of debt from his master, the servant failed to pass on such forgiveness of debt—in a comparatively trifling matter—to a fellow servant.) Reconciled with God through the costly love of Christ, believers are obligated henceforth to live out and extend that reconciliation to others.

Characteristically, Paul does not leave the appeal for reconciliation there but reinforces it with yet another formulation of God's act in Christ. The statement is one that is perhaps the most theologically daring of anything he has written:

> For our sake he made him who knew no sin into
> sin, so that in him we might become the righteous-
> ness of God. (v. 21)

This is one of a number of what have been called "interchange" statements that Paul makes in regard to the redemptive mission of Christ: Christ becomes what we are, so that we might share what he is. Later in the letter, Paul puts it in terms of riches and poverty:

> For you know the generous act of our Lord Jesus
> Christ, that though he was rich, yet for your sakes
> he became poor, so that by his poverty you might
> become rich. (2 Cor 8:9)

The "richness" stated here in relation to Christ hardly refers to any material riches he or his family enjoyed during his earthly life; there is no suggestion in the gospels that Jesus came from a wealthy family. The "richness" in question is that mentioned in the first stanza of the Philippians hymn: the "equality with God" that he enjoyed in his pre-temporal existence with God and which he did not regard as something to exploit for personal gain; on the contrary, becoming incarnate, he "emptied himself" of such richness, taking on the poverty of the human condition in the most extreme sense, that of a slave (Phil 2:6–8).

Here (2 Cor 5:21), though, Christ's entrance into and identification with the human condition is expressed more radically still. Paul has no doubts about the personal sinlessness of Christ ("who knew no sin") but states that God made him, who knew no sin, "into sin." How should we interpret that last phrase "into sin"? Within the "interchange" pattern previously noted, the thought would seem to be that Christ has exchanged the sinlessness proper to his own person as Divine Son for the condition in terms of relationship to God consequent upon human sin. As representative of the entire human race, he has taken upon himself the sin-burden of the race and the alienation from God consequent upon it. Again, as representative of the race, he has overcome that burden and alienation through the supreme act of love expressed in his obedient death on the cross. In union with him ("in him"), then, sinful human beings can take advantage of the "justification," the verdict of acquittal that his obedience and self-sacrificial love have gained.

Paul expresses this new reality in a striking final clause. He does not write, as we might have expected, "so that in him we might become righteous [*dikaioi*]" but something far stronger: "so that in him we might become the righteousness [*dikaiosynē*] of God." "Righteousness" is a technical term of the Pauline tradition. It is a biblical concept not all that easily expressed in theological or spiritual discourse today. Basically, *righteousness* means faithfulness to the requirements of a relationship, a faithfulness shown in action. What Paul understands and describes God to be doing in Christ is acting faithfully as Creator—of the world and of humankind within the world—to rescue the world from the plight that it has got itself into through sin. In his costly entrance into the depths of human alienation from God in order to effect this rescue, Christ is the veritable embodiment of this divine faithfulness to the world, this divine "righteousness" (see also Rom 3:21–26).

For Paul, in responding through faith and baptism to the divine initiative proclaimed in the gospel, human beings do not acquire a righteousness of their own. Rather, they are, as it were, "built into" the divine righteousness embodied in Christ. In him as the "image" of God (2 Cor 3:18; 4:4–6), they acquire—or "re-acquire"—the responsibility for the remainder of creation that God bestowed on human beings on the sixth day of the Creation.

This sense of participating in the faithfulness of God to the world is one of the engines driving Paul's mission. Christian life is not just about being "righteous" or virtuous in a static way, ordered apart from or away from the world. Rather, it means being turned toward the world as the outreach of divine faithfulness, offering to the world, as Paul says in Philippians, "the word of life" (Phil 2:16).

In light of this grand vision of the mission in which he and his coworkers are engaged, Paul urges the Corinthians "not to accept the grace of God in vain" (6:1). The "day of salvation" (Isa 49:8) is not over and done with. It remains to be lived out in a continuing "Now!" (6:2), a perpetual conversion of heart.

SUGGESTED SCRIPTURE

Romans 5:6–11; 6:1–14; Ephesians 2:11–22; Matthew 18:23–25 (parable of the unforgiving servant)

DAY 3

PERSONAL REFLECTION

What does this passage communicate to me about the Father?

Can I say, with Paul, that "the love of Christ overwhelms me"?

What does it mean for me to live now, no longer for myself, but for the one (Christ) who died and was raised for me?

To what extent do I live out the reconciliation I, myself, have received from God?

Am I being called to be an "ambassador" for Christ? How might this change my life if it were so?

What are the implications of "becoming the righteousness of God"—for myself, for others, for the world in which I live?

Briefly, how is this time (of retreat) a "Now" of salvation for me?

DAY 4

———◦◦◦———

CONVERSION AND CALL

We have been considering how Paul presents his apostolic mission as a summons to people to be reconciled with God (2 Cor 6:1–2). Behind the power of his appeal in this regard was his own personal experience of reconciliation with God. Let us now explore his discovery of the God of grace on the road to Damascus.

PAUL'S CONVERSION ACCORDING TO THE ACTS OF THE APOSTLES

Acts informs us that Paul was a man of the Jewish Diaspora, from a family living in Tarsus, "no mean city" (Acts 21:39), situated in the rich Roman province of Cilicia. Among other advantages, Tarsus enjoyed a reputation for the quality of its academies. Paul's later facility in Greek and knowledge of popular philosophy and literature suggest that he benefited from this environment, growing up a person of two worlds: the Jewish biblical and the Greco-Roman, with some facility to move culturally back and forth between them. At some stage in his youth, perhaps just out of his teens, he seems to have felt the call to go to Palestine and there deepen his knowledge of his ancestral faith.

There is a certain irony in Paul's claim, according to Acts 22:3, to have sat at the feet of the Jewish teacher, Gamaliel. Gamaliel was famous for the mildness of his interpretations of the Law. Paul, by his own admission, tells us that, having adhered to the sect of the Pharisees, he advanced beyond all his contemporaries in his zeal for the *minutiae* of the Law and, in particular, the preservation of the "traditions" by which members of that party adapted the ancient Law to the contemporary situation (Gal 1:13–14). In short, Paul became something of a religious fanatic—a type all too evident in our world today. Fanatical zeal for the Law led him into a short but very sharp and injurious career as persecutor of a movement newly arisen within Judaism. The adherents of this movement, later known as "Christians" (Acts 11:26), claimed that Jesus of Nazareth, who had been crucified by the Romans a few years earlier, on the charge of being a messianic pretender to the throne of David, was in fact the Messiah of Israel and revealed Son of God.

It is often maintained, surely with some plausibility, that people who engage in the persecution of others for deviance from some accepted norm, are actually attempting to suppress their own subconscious doubts about their identity and the validity of that norm. Whether Paul's persecuting activity was similarly reactive to doubts rising within him is hard to tell. There have been attempts to psychologize him, but the evidence is limited and the results speculative. There is no doubt, however, that his own sense of identity was deeply bound up with adherence to Judaism and to the "perfection" with which he attempted to live out the tenets of the Law according to the most rigorous Pharisaic interpretation (Phil 3:4–6). In a sense, Paul was a convert to an extreme form of

Judaism before he became a convert to faith in Jesus as the Messiah.

The experience that happened to him on the road to Damascus, according to Acts, must be accounted one of the great personal turn-arounds in history—both in itself and in the vast scale of the consequences it set in train. Acts provides no less than three accounts of Paul's conversion—the first is a third-person description (9:1–22), whereas the second (22:3–16) and third (26:4–23) are personal accounts from Paul. Why, we might well ask, did Luke devote so much space to this event, telling it three times, in very much the same terms, when surely there was a lot more information to convey about the early years of the church that later generations would have been glad to receive? It is, in fact, a characteristic of Luke to describe things repeatedly. An even more elaborate example would be the interaction between Peter and the Roman centurion, Cornelius, that led to the community's acceptance that Gentiles, previously considered "unclean," were being called into the Christian community (Acts 10:1—11:19). Luke includes these repeated accounts in order to drive home a point: if God's grace was powerful enough to confront a life going so strongly in one direction and turn it around to make it the most effective instrument for furthering all that it had previously opposed, so God's grace was strong enough to overcome all opposition to the spread of the gospel, especially that arising from religious and ethnic identity.

Distinctive in Luke's account is the self-identification of the risen one whom Paul encounters in the terrifying vision: "Saul, Saul, why are you persecuting me?" (v. 4); "I am Jesus, whom you are persecuting" (v. 5). Instantly, these words communicate something that became integral to Paul's theology: the identification of the risen Lord with the community of believers, who constitute his extended person or "body" (see 1 Cor 12:12–13; Rom 12:4–5). Immediately, the encounter results in action and mission: "Get up! Go into the city. You will be told what it is that you must do" (Acts 9:6). Helpless, blind, and needing to be led by hand, this hitherto energetic young man must spend some days sitting in darkness, praying, unable to eat, waiting, until finally, by means of a greeting as "brother," the laying-on of hands, the pouring of water in baptism, he is brought into the community of those he had once hated and persecuted.

We see here a classic instance of a motif often found in Luke where one person or party has a deep experience of God while at the same time another person or party—in this case, Ananias—has a separate but complementary one. Then both parties come together, so that individual experience becomes community experience and is greatly deepened thereby.[1] That is, God calls Ananias to overcome his fear and prejudice against Saul, and to minister to him the welcome, healing, instruction and rites that will make him a member of the community of believers. In this way, Saul's conversion amounts to something more than the extraordinary experience of an individual. The community, in the person of Ananias, works with God to minister to Saul. It also has its own identity and knowledge of divine power broadened by the inclusion of this extraordinary new member.

PAUL'S OWN ACCOUNTS OF HIS CONVERSION AND CALL

Let us now turn to passages from Paul's own writings that reflect his discovery of Christ. The first is really just a reference in a subordinate clause early in Galatians, but it goes to the heart of the matter:

> You have heard, no doubt, of my earlier life in Judaism. I was violently persecuting the church of God

and was trying to destroy it. I advanced in Judaism beyond many among my people of the same age, for I was far more zealous for the traditions of my ancestors. But when God, who had set me apart before I was born and called me through his grace, was pleased to reveal his Son to me, so that I might proclaim him among the Gentiles, I did not confer with any human being, nor did I go up to Jerusalem to those who were already apostles before me, but I went away at once into Arabia, and afterwards I returned to Damascus. (Gal 1:13–17)

You will notice here Paul's frank acknowledgment of the intensity of his allegiance to his ancestral religion and the zeal for the traditions that led him to "violently persecute" the church of God and seek to destroy it. But then comes the all-important "when…" clause that contains so much. First, there is the prophetic consciousness, echoing the language of the call of prophets such as Jeremiah (1:5) and (Second) Isaiah (49:1), that God had "set him apart" before he was born. This reflects Paul's conviction that his whole life—although we could say *every* human life—is grasped even before it comes into existence within the saving plan of God. Then there is the phrase "called me through his grace." "Call" is a rich concept in Paul's usage. He associates "call" with the divine act of creation (Rom 4:17; 9:24–26). People are "called into being," "called out of nothingness" into existence and relationship with God. More precisely, Paul associates "calling" with the moment of conversion, when a person aligns their life with the pretemporal design of God in their regard and begins from then on to follow the pattern of life that God seems to be setting out before them (see 1 Cor 1:26; 7:17–24). This sense of "vocation," to put it in language we more commonly use, does not necessarily mean that one is given then and there a detailed divine blueprint to follow. One is called, as

Ignatius would probably agree, to commit oneself to a life of growing intimacy with God in which, through lifelong discernment, divine grace will lead the way.

As Paul indicates, his call began with a "revelation" of God's Son (Gal 1:16). Jesus of Nazareth, the one whom the Romans had crucified as a messianic pretender, concerning whom deluded followers had been making claims utterly blasphemous in terms of Jewish faith, was now revealed to him as indeed God's Son. The face of the Crucified One—which Paul could readily imagine, even if, as would seem to have been the case, he was not present at the crucifixion—was revealed to him as in some sense the face of God.

It is hard for us to grasp the challenge to Paul's previous image of God represented by this revelation. Another brief passage—this time in 2 Corinthians 4—gives an attractive hint of what was involved:

> And even if our gospel is veiled, it is veiled to those who are perishing. In their case the god of this world has blinded the minds of the unbelievers, to keep them from seeing [what believers see:] the light of the gospel of the glory of Christ, who is the image of God. For we do not proclaim ourselves; we proclaim Jesus Christ as Lord and ourselves as your slaves for Jesus' sake. For it is the God who said, "*Let light shine out of darkness,*" who has shone in our hearts to give the light of the knowledge of the glory of God in the face of Jesus Christ. (2 Cor 4:3–6)

Notice, in particular, that final sentence: "It is the God who said, '*Let light shine out of darkness.*'" This can only be a reference to the first act of Creation (Gen 1:3). It is, then, God as Creator who has shone light in the darkness of unbelieving hearts. This light, shone on the face of the Crucified One, reveals it to be no longer the tortured visage of a failed messianic pretender but the very image of God (v. 4), the "glory of God" (v. 6). We are back with the Christology of the Christ-hymn in Philippians: Christ is the "image" of God, as Adam was meant to be the image of God and meant to pass on that likeness to God to all his descendants. In the face of Adam's failure, the crucified Christ images God by revealing the essence of God to be the self-emptying love displayed in the Crucified One. We recall Paul's personal conviction of this truth in Galatians: "[Christ], who loved me and delivered himself up for me" in response to that love (2:20). So drastic was the change in Paul's view of Jesus of Nazareth and the image of God revealed in his death that Paul regards it as an extension of God's work of creation.

Notice that here in 2 Corinthians, Paul is speaking in the plural. The experience is not unique to him. It is part of all Christian conversion, a conversion that is not a once-off event but the beginning of a process. A couple of sentences at the end of the preceding chapter put this superbly:

> Now the Lord is the Spirit, and where the Spirit of the Lord is, there is freedom. And all of us, with unveiled faces, seeing as in a mirror the glory of the Lord are being transformed into the same image from one degree of glory to another; for this comes from the Lord, the Spirit. (2 Cor 3:17–18)

These two sentences come at the end of a long sequence where Paul has been contrasting the ministry of "slavery" that he associates with Moses and the Law, with the ministry of "freedom" that he associates with the Spirit. We will return to this contrast between the Law and the Spirit later on. For the present, let us note Paul's understanding that Christian life involves an ongoing, "unveiled" contemplation of the "glory" or likeness to God that is "reflected" for us in the "mirror" that is the risen Lord, who, we may assume, for Paul as well as for Luke (24:39) and John (20:20, 27), still bears on his body the wounds that are the marks of his love.

Note also that this "contemplation" of God in the mirror that is Christ is not static but something effecting transformation. We are being "transformed into the same image from one degree of glory to another," through the work of the Spirit. Christian life involves—or should involve—a continual transformation into greater and greater likeness to Christ as "image of God"—as Paul puts it, from one degree of glory to another. The original design of the Creator for human beings—that they should live out the "likeness to God" in which they were created (Gen 1:26–28)—is finally being realized in the New Adam, who, as Paul says elsewhere, "became a life-giving Spirit" (1 Cor 15:45).

Finally, before leaving Paul's own accounts of his conversion and call, let us note the divine intent that he saw in it according to the brief allusion in Galatians:

> But when God…was pleased to reveal his Son to me, so that I might proclaim him among the Gentiles. (Gal 1:15–16)

The last clause indicates the apostolic purpose of Paul's vocation. Scholars dispute whether Paul received both his conversion and his specific mission to be apostle to the Gentiles at one and the same moment or whether the latter mission developed following some years of preaching initially to his fellow Jews—as, in fact, Acts suggests (see 9:20–22). Whatever the case, it is undeniable that his distinctive concern to summon the nations of the world into the community of believers was intimately bound up with the dramatic recasting of his vision of God that conversion to the crucified Messiah involved. God did not shed his grace exclusively or even principally on those who lived righteously according to the Law. God's characteristic impulse was to seek out and find the lost, the distant, the alienated, and invite them to reconciliation—the same pattern, of course, displayed in the ministry of Jesus (Matt 9:13; Mark 2:17; Luke 5:32; 19:10).

PAUL, SERVANT OF THE MYSTERY OF CHRIST (EPH 3:1-13)

Paul's sense of having a specific call in relation to the Gentiles receives a most attractive reflection midway through the Letter to the Ephesians. The truth that Jesus Christ is not only the Messiah of Israel but also the one through whom the nations of the world, as "co-heirs" of Israel, are to have a share in the "riches" of salvation is described here as the "mystery" of Christ (3:5). This mystery, hidden from all eternity in the wisdom of God, has only recently been revealed through the Spirit "to his holy apostles and prophets" (3:5). Paul, who has been given a specific revelation of this mystery (v. 2), sees himself as the particular "minister" (*diakonos*) of the gospel in which this mystery is proclaimed:

> Of this gospel I have become a minister according to the gift of God's grace that was given me by the working of his power. Although I am the very least of all the saints, this grace was given to me to bring to the Gentiles the news of the inexhaustible riches of Christ, and to make everyone see what is the plan of the mystery hidden for ages in God who created all things; so that through the church the wisdom of God in its rich variety might now be made known to the rulers and authorities in the heavenly places. (Eph 3:7–10)

Two phrases in this passage are particularly worthy of comment. Paul refers to "the inexhaustible riches of Christ" (v. 8). "Inexhaustible" translates a rare Greek term, *anexichniaston*. This is often rendered "inscrutable" or "unfathomable" in the sense of being beyond the capacity of human knowledge (see Rom 11:33). A more literal understanding is preferable here. Paul means that the "riches," that is, the saving benefits contained in Christ, are so vast as to be literally inexhaustible— like a gold or silver mine that is never exhausted, no matter how deeply its shafts or tunnels are run. The thought is close to that of Colossians 1:27 ("the riches of the glory of this mystery, which is Christ in you, the hope of glory") and 2:2– 3 ("Christ himself, in whom are hidden all the treasures of wisdom and knowledge"). Where once the benefits of the Messiah seemed destined for Israel alone, their richness is now clearly of such inexhaustible scope as to be available to the entire world. This is the "treasure" that Paul and his fellow workers carry in the fragile "clay vessels" of their mortal bodies (2 Cor 4:7). This is why, though "poor," they are "making many rich," why, though having "nothing," they "possess everything" (2 Cor 6:10; see also 1 Cor 3:23).

The second notable phrase in the passage makes up most of verse 10: "So that through the church the wisdom of God in all its rich variety might be made known to the rulers and authorities in the heavenly places." "All its rich variety" renders a Greek adjective *peripoikilos*, which, in a slightly simpler form, is used in the Greek translation (LXX) of Genesis to describe Joseph's "coat of many colors" (37:3). The thought seems to be that the church—made up now of Jewish and Gentile believers, in which also other key differences, social and gender (see Gal 3:28) are of no account—displays and models to the spiritual powers that held the old, passing creation in thrall the possibility of a new humanity coming into being through Christ. This vision of God's power and Christ's inexhaustible riches lies behind and drives Paul's mission to the nations of the world.

REFLECTION

On this account, we can say that it is the "Gentile" regions of our hearts and our lives, the sinful, the wounded, the unloved, and unlovable, that particularly attract God's attention and healing grace. It is a mistake to hide them from God—or from our confessors or spiritual directors—though that, according to good Ignatian teaching, is precisely what the bad spirit will seek to achieve ("Rules for Discernment," *Spiritual Exercises*, §326).

SUGGESTED SCRIPTURE

Psalms 31 (32); 34 (35); Acts 9:1–22; 22:3–16; 26:4–23; 2 Corinthians 3:18—4:6; 4:7–15; Galatians 1:11–24; Ephesians 3:1–21; 1 Timothy 1:12–17

PERSONAL REFLECTION

Reflecting on my life:
> Can I discern significant moments of "conversion"?
> Did any such moment alter in any way my image of God?
> Can I identify anything that might have led up to any such moment?
> Did any new direction or "mission" in my life emerge?
> Is God shining a light in my heart in any way at the present time?

INSTRUMENT OF GOD'S GRACE

We have been considering Paul's discovery of God as a God of grace—not only to Israel, and to Paul personally, but also to the nations of the world. We will now consider some passages that strongly display Paul's conviction of being powerfully grasped and energized by God's grace.

First, a word about "grace," which is so significant for Paul—and which his premier interpreter, St. Augustine of Hippo, developed so richly for the later church. "Grace," of course, is the English translation of the Greek term, *charis*. *Charis* most basically denotes the charm or attractiveness of a person who spontaneously wins the favor of others. When a person with *charis* walks into a room, immediately all eyes turn to her or him, followed by glances of approval. Reciprocally, then, it denotes the favor and goodwill created in other persons through such charm. More concretely, *charis* can refer to a gift bestowed on a person as an expression of such favor.

In Old Testament usage, the Greek term *charis* picks up the Hebrew word *hēn* in much the same sense—especially in respect to the favor of God bestowed on human beings, with or without their doing anything to merit it (as in "Noah found favor in the eyes of the Lord" [Gen 6:8]). In the New Testament, the sense of unmerited divine favor predominates. Although the world did not in any sense possess "charm" or grace, God chose to regard it with favor and sent the Son on a mission to draw human beings into the transforming power of divine grace. Paul sees the entire sending and work of Christ as the spearpoint of an immense wave of God's grace flowing over a sinful world, seeking to reconcile that world to its Creator (2 Cor 5:18—6:2; Rom 5:15). Paul understands his conversion on the road to Damascus as a radical experience of being grasped by God's grace, so that henceforth his entire life and energy becomes an instrument of that grace to the wider world. His apostolic calling is a gift (*charis*) in the sense of a specific concrete expression of God's grace toward him personally (Rom 1:5; 15:15; 1 Cor 3:10; Gal 2:9).

ENCOUNTER WITH THE RISEN LORD AND INSTRUMENT OF GRACE (1 COR 15:8–10)

Paul writes of being energized by God's grace with particular intensity toward the end of the celebrated text where he reminds the Corinthians of the bedrock on which their faith in the resurrection rests:

> For I handed on to you as of first importance what I in turn had received: that Christ died for our sins in accordance with the scriptures, and that he was buried, and that he was raised on the third day in accordance with the scriptures, and that he appeared to Cephas, then to the twelve. Then he appeared to more than five hundred brothers and sisters at one time, most of whom are still alive, though some have died. Then he appeared to James, then to all the apostles. Last of all, as the one untimely born [*ektrōma*], he appeared also to me. For I am the least of the apostles, unfit to be called an apostle, because I persecuted the church of God. But by the grace of God I am what I am, and his grace toward me has not been in vain. On the contrary, I worked harder than any of them—though it was not I, but the grace of God that is with me. Whether then it was I or they, so we proclaim and so you have come to believe. (1 Cor 15:3–11)

It is generally agreed that in the opening lines of this text, Paul is in fact quoting a very early Christian creed that he had passed on to the Corinthians when he first drew them to Christ. Where exactly the creedal fragment ends and Paul's own list of the resurrection witnesses takes over is not clear. He is certainly freely composing when he finally arrives at himself as the last to receive an appearance of the risen Lord (v. 8).

With reference to himself as last of the Easter witnesses, Paul employs the striking term *ektrōma*. This word has a range of meaning in ancient medical usage under the general rubric of a birth that is abnormal or out of the usual time sequence. It can refer to a miscarriage, an abortion, or an induced birth. Paul seems to mean that, if one looks on the resurrection witnesses as siblings within a family, he is the last one, the unexpected one, the one whose birth is not natural or even—if a miscarriage is in view—one that required the creative power of God. Personally, I think the sense of "induced birth" is the most suitable. Unlike the other witnesses—Peter and the rest of the Twelve, for example—Paul had not been a disciple of Jesus. On the contrary, his life and career had been going in a diametrically opposite direction: he was persecuting Jesus in the persons of his followers. That *he* would become a believer was the last thing anyone would have expected. It required, then, a far greater effort on the part of God's grace to turn his life around and bring him to birth as a believer, a key resurrection witness, and an apostle set apart for a specific mission to the nations of the world.

Notice the three references to "the grace of God" in verse 10 (author's emphasis):

> But by the *grace* of God I am what I am, and his *grace* toward me has not been in vain. On the contrary,

I worked harder than any of them—though it was
not I, but the *grace* of God that is with me.

Here, the understanding of God's grace is not simply that
of divine favor in a detached sense. Grace has become a
force that is driving and energizing Paul's apostolic work.
Or perhaps we should say that Paul has been swept into the
wider stream of God's grace that has flowed into the world in
the mission of Christ. To make the point, Paul indulges for a
moment in a boast: he has "worked harder than all of them,"
that is, than all the remaining apostles. Here, as so often in
Paul, "work" has the technical meaning of being on mission to
proclaim the gospel and found local communities of believers
(churches). Paul seems to let slip a feeling that, while he was
wearing himself out on far-flung and dangerous missions
across the Mediterranean world, some of the other apostles
were just sitting around in Jerusalem or elsewhere enjoying
the status of apostle but not doing much else. Immediately,
however, he corrects himself and says, "Though it was not I
but the grace of God that is with me."

Paul thinks of the grace of God as targeting him even
before he was born and then, at the right moment, swooping
down to grasp his life, turn it in a totally opposite direction,
and make him the key instrument for the extension of grace
throughout the world. While his role is undoubtedly unique,
he would agree that every human life is similarly grasped by
divine grace from beginning to end. Although the language
differs, the same insight is fundamental to the "Rules for Discernment of Spirits" in the *Spiritual Exercises*, whereby a person is taught to be sensitive to the tugs of the good spirit in
the direction of responding to grace, away from the deceit
and confusion sown by the bad spirit.

CAPTURED BY CHRIST (PHIL 3:2–11)

The Letter to the Philippians provides an equally vivid account of the radical turnaround in Paul's life when he was "captured" by Christ. It occurs at a point in the letter where the warmhearted exhortation to this beloved community takes a sudden turn in the direction of a warning to be on the lookout against people he describes in very negative terms:

> Beware of the dogs, beware of the evil workers, beware of those who mutilate the flesh! (3:2)

Paul issues this sharp warning to preserve the community at Philippi, after his likely demise, from being "got at" in the way that the churches in Galatia were got at by missionaries of a more legalistic cast stemming from Jerusalem. Though themselves believers in Christ, these intruders into Paul's Gentile churches were insisting that to be members of God's people destined for salvation, believers from the Gentile world had to take on the full yoke of the Mosaic Law, especially circumcision for males. As Paul made clear in angry tones in Galatians, this is to frustrate God's design for the Gentiles and, above all, to nullify the value of Christ's costly death (Gal 2:21). It is the latter consideration, in particular, that accounts for the passion expressed in Philippians, where Paul speaks of his own conversion as a model for all believers who, like him, have been "captured" by Christ for the new creation:

> For it is we who are the circumcision, who worship in the Spirit of God and boast in Christ Jesus and have no confidence in the flesh—even though I, too, have reason for confidence in the flesh. If anyone else has reason to be confident in the flesh, I have more: circumcised on the eighth day, a member

of the people of Israel, of the tribe of Benjamin, a
Hebrew born of Hebrews; as to the law, a Pharisee;
as to zeal, a persecutor of the church; as to righteousness under the law, blameless. (Phil 3:3–6)

Paul lists here, on no less than seven grounds, his impeccable
Jewish credentials—not just as a Jew, but as a most zealous
and perfect keeper of the Law. These are all the things on
which he invested his identity in the old era, all the grounds
for confidence of right standing before God ("righteousness")
that he had to surrender when coming to faith in Christ.

To drive the point home, Paul has recourse to an
"accounting" image that he sometimes uses (see also Rom
4:4–5)—that of a balance sheet, where losses are indicated on
one column and gains on the opposite. All those privileges
and achievements that he previously listed on the "gain" or
"profit" side of the ledger, he has now transferred to the "loss"
side—and done so happily because a tremendous new "gain"
has intervened:

Yet whatever gains I had, these I have come to
regard as loss because of Christ. More than that,
I regard everything as loss because of the surpassing value of knowing Christ Jesus my Lord. For
his sake I have suffered the loss of all things, and
I regard them as rubbish [*skybala*], in order that I
may gain Christ and be found in him, not having
a righteousness of my own that comes from the
law, but one that comes through faith in Christ, the
righteousness from God based on faith. (vv. 7–9)

The gain has so relativized his previous credentials as to
render them by comparison not only "loss" (in the accounting
sense mentioned above) but "rubbish," "garbage," material

of no value that you would throw away. (The Greek word *skybala* is strong, even offensive!)

And Paul proceeds in a way that brings out the utterly christocentric focus of his life and spirituality from the moment of initial transformation:

> I want to know Christ and the power of his resurrection and the sharing of his sufferings by becoming like him in his death, if somehow I may attain the resurrection from the dead. (vv. 10–11)

Paul's desire to "know" Christ has the Semitic nuance where "knowing" goes beyond intellectual knowledge to connote experience as well. He has in mind the same deeply "intimate" knowledge that Ignatius speaks of in the grace to be asked for in the contemplations of the Second Week of the Exercises: "To ask for an interior knowledge of our Lord, Who for me has become incarnate, that I may the more love Him and follow Him" (*Spiritual Exercises*, §104). Knowing Christ in this intimate way means knowing the "power of his resurrection" in the sharing of his suffering. It is in the weakness of suffering with Christ that one experiences most strongly the power that will lead to resurrection, a theme Paul develops at length in 2 Corinthians 4:7–14. Writing in this vein, Paul is doubtless very conscious of the fate that may well lie ahead of him in the coming weeks—even days. He is confident that the more intensely he is united with Christ in suffering, the more certainly he will share his resurrection.

RUNNING IN THE RACE (PHIL 3:12–14)

The following verses (vv. 12–14) introduce something of a correction or clarification, and also a fresh image: that of the "race" familiar to Paul's readers from the athletic contests regularly held in the cities of the Greco-Roman world:

> Not that I have already obtained this or have already reached the goal; but I press on to capture it, just as I have been captured by Christ Jesus. Beloved, I do not consider that I have captured it; but this one thing I do: forgetting what lies behind and straining forward to what lies ahead, I press on toward the goal for the prize of the upward call of God in Christ Jesus. (vv. 12–14)

What Paul is at pains to indicate here is his sense of still running in the race—the race to eternal life. He is not at the starting point—and certainly not behind it, as would be the case if he were still living and striving for perfection according to the Mosaic Law. But he still hasn't breasted the finishing tape. He presses on to "capture" it, as Christ Jesus has "captured" him. The Greek verb *katalambanein*, rendered here as "capture," is usually translated by softer expressions such as "obtain" (NIV) or "make [one's] own" (NRSV). These scarcely do justice to the vigor of the Greek, which conveys the sense of catching something or someone suddenly, as a parent might grab hold of a child walking on the sidewalk of a busy street if the child ventures out toward the edge. Paul's language well conveys the sense of how the risen Lord "captured" him on the road to Damascus and turned his life in a totally opposite direction to the one in which he was going.

The present task is to press on to the "prize of the upward call" from God (v. 14). Within the continuing image of the race, the "upward call" refers to the herald's summons to the winning athlete to mount the dais to receive the victor's wreath. Paul is thinking of the "upward call" as sharing in the exaltation of Christ as risen Lord. For the moment, however, he is still very much on the way—flinging the past behind him, straining to cover the remaining track to the finishing line.

A THORN IN THE FLESH (2 COR 12:7-10)

In this connection, it is worth noting a mysterious allusion that Paul makes in another letter to what he calls a "thorn in the flesh, a messenger of Satan to torment me, to keep me from being too elated" (2 Cor 12:7). What Paul means by "a thorn in the flesh" has defied explanation. In the polemical context of this part of 2 Corinthians (chapters 10—13), he is hardly referring to some moral failing. More likely, "the thorn" is some chronic disfigurement or disability that renders his presence unattractive or less effectual in some way.[2] Again and again, Paul asked the Lord to rid him of it (v. 8) but received the response, "My grace is sufficient for you, for power is made perfect in weakness" (v. 9). So he concludes with the following:

> Therefore I am content with weaknesses, insults, hardships, persecutions, and calamities for the sake of Christ; for whenever I am weak, then I am strong. (v. 10)

Not only the trials and labors of apostolic work (see 2 Cor 11:21–33) but even this form of personal weakness provided greater scope for God's grace, leading to the conclusion: "When I am weak, then I am strong." This sentiment built into Paul's personal spirituality complements the sense of being "on the way" so strikingly brought out in the passage from Philippians 3. Since grace builds on nature, our strengths can be assets in the work of God. At the same time, they can arm us against the subtler prompting of divine grace. Our weaknesses and imperfections, on the other hand, can disarm our resistance and lead us to cast ourselves more fully and trustingly on the power of God.

REFLECTION

This sense of being "on the way"—not back in the past, not yet arrived—is central to Pauline spirituality—and indeed central to all sound spirituality. So much spiritual direction is concerned with setting people free from things that imprison them in their *past*: guilts, angers, resentments, feelings of failure. So much is equally concerned with getting people free from paralyzing thoughts and feelings about the *future*: fears and anxieties about what might happen or be required of them. A similar discouragement stemming from the future would be a tendency to impose on themselves a "perfection" at which they have not yet arrived: demands and expectations that belong to the future and are too much for the present. So much direction, then, consists of getting people to be where they are at present, that is, "on the way," moving beyond the captivities of the past, while not allowing a false anticipation of the future to paralyze choices here and now.[3] As Ignatius teaches, the bad spirit is a past master at exploiting the human tendency to live in past or future in these ways so as to disturb the peaceful "walk" with God that should characterize present Christian life. It is all part of the "lie," the "deception" that has been the hallmark of temptation from the start. The good spirit, on the contrary will always take a person to the reality of the "now": not in the past, not yet arrived but, like Paul, "on the way."

SUGGESTED SCRIPTURE

1 Corinthians 15:3–11; Philippians 3:3–14; 2 Corinthians 4:7–15; 11:21—12:12; Galatians 6:14–18; 2 Timothy 4:6–8

PERSONAL REFLECTION

Do I see myself as grasped by God's grace?

In what ways am I an instrument of God's grace?

In good works, do I say, "Not I, but the grace of God that is with me"?

Is my relationship with God held hostage to anything stemming from my past?

Am I paralyzed in some way by fears or anxieties about the future?

Do I demand a false "perfection" of myself or others?

What does it mean for me to be "on the way"—living the here and now?

Has some "weakness" led me to a greater experience of the power of divine grace?

DAY 5

---◦⟨≫⟩◦---

THE HOPE THAT SPRINGS FROM GOD'S LOVE

We have been considering the sharp warning Paul gave to the Philippians about being on their guard against intrusive teachers or missionaries who might try to take them back under the yoke of the Jewish law (Phil 3:2–14). We saw how Paul, appealing to the image of a race, outlines the situation he regards himself and all believers to be in at the present time: still "on the way" to salvation, well beyond the start but not yet arrived at the finish. We noted how important this understanding of present Christian existence was for Paul's spirituality and that it also featured prominently in the pastoral direction he gave to his communities. Let us now trace this "on the way" sense of Christian life more intensively, paying particular attention to central chapters of the Letter to the Romans.

First, a word about this great letter, which is generally reckoned to be Paul's masterwork, and certainly the one that has had the most profound impact on the Christian tradition. What sets it apart from other Pauline letters is the fact that it was written to a community that Paul had not himself founded, although one that he intended to visit en route to new apostolic pastures in Spain (Rom 15:24, 28). When writing to his own communities, Paul can presume knowledge of the basic gospel and concentrate on its implications for particular aspects of Christian life. In Romans, however, he expounds the gospel at length, so that, before his arrival, the community of believers in Rome will have a firsthand account of what he proclaims and teaches, and so be prepared to support his mission to the West.[1]

BECOMING "RIGHT WITH GOD" THROUGH FAITH (ROM 1—4)

In the first four chapters of the letter, after the introduction (1:1–15), Paul basically shows how, in the light of what God has done in Christ—sending a crucified Messiah— "justification" or coming into right relationship with God cannot be based on the practice of the Law. The universal prevalence of sin means that it must be available on the basis of divine grace and a human response resting solely on faith. If justification were on the basis of the Law, then it would apply only to those who possessed the Law, namely, Jews. Paul, on the other hand, sees God's action in Christ as reaching out beyond Israel to embrace the nations of the world, offering justification simply on the basis of faith.

At stake here is a distinctive vision of God: a God who acts graciously and inclusively, rather than exclusively and on the basis of merit. Paul privileges the covenant God made with Abraham over the later covenant God made with Moses. He does so because the former covenant is open and universalizing, whereas the latter is exclusive, restricting salvation to a particular nation, the Jews. Did not God promise Abraham, "In you and your seed all the nations of the world will be blessed" (Gen 12:2; 22:18)? If God is, as the Scriptures of Israel proclaim from the very start, the Creator of the entire world rather

92

than just the covenant partner of Israel, then God must have a concern for the entire world, not just for Israel (Rom 3:27–30). Is it not Israel's distinctive vocation as a people to hold the promises of God in trust until the right time for them to be extended to the nations of the world (Rom 4:16–18)?

Faith is the essential human response to this revelation of God. Faith acknowledges that I am part of that sinful mass of humanity that stands in need of rescue by the gracious outreach of God in the person and life of Jesus.[2] It is in line with this that every liturgical celebration of the Eucharist begins with a confession that we are sinners in need of God's mercy and forgiveness. Sometimes it seems a rather negative way to begin the liturgy, especially if the celebrant follows the set formula starkly without preliminary introduction of some kind. Yet it is an expression of faith, aligning us in right relationship to the God of grace before we begin the central act of worship that enacts our identity as Christians.

Faith in this sense, faith in the God of grace who in the person of the Son has reached out to us as sinners, is what draws us into right relationship with God and keeps us there: what "justifies" us, to use Paul's technical language. In this connection, we can think once again of Jesus' parable of the Pharisee and the tax collector (Luke 18:9–14). The Pharisee who spent his time in the Temple reminding God of all his good works, and to make the point more strongly, looked sideways and contrasted himself with the "sinner" down the back, did not go down to his house afterward "at rights with God, or "justified," whereas the tax collector, who simply prayed, "God, be merciful to me, a sinner," did go down justified in God's eyes.

THE HOPE OF GLORY (ROM 5:1–11)

With the principle of "justification by faith" established in this way, Paul is ready by the end of chapter 4 to begin a new section of Romans (chapters 5—8). The section begins with something like a great sign of relief:

> Justified then by faith, we have peace with God through our Lord Jesus Christ, through whom we have obtained access to this grace in which we stand; and we boast in our hope of sharing the glory of God. (5:1–2)

"Justified then by faith" is a clear statement that puts the past firmly behind us. We are in right relationship with God; we have "peace" with God. "Peace" foreshadows the motif of "reconciliation" that will surface explicitly a few verses further on and which, of course, we have already seen in 2 Corinthians 5:18–20. With this past of "enmity" with God behind us, we are in a totally new situation: we have "access to the grace—the divine good favor—in which we stand" and look now to the future: "our hope of sharing the glory of God." The focus on "faith" that dominated the first four chapters is now giving way to the second virtue in Paul's triad of "faith," "hope," and "love" (see 1 Cor 13:13).

The hope is that of "sharing the glory of God." "Glory" runs like a golden thread throughout Romans, surfacing in almost every chapter. "Glory" (*doxa*) in Paul is closely associated with "image" (*eikōn*). Human beings, created in the image and likeness of God, were meant as such to participate in God's glory: to reflect the divine image before the remainder of creation (Gen 1:26–28; Ps 8:3–8). Sin radically tarnished that God-likeness or glory, but Christ, as the "New" or "Last Adam," has come into the world truly imaging God. As such, he has recreated the possibility of human beings displaying the glory intended to be our dignity and destiny from the start. Returning for a moment to 2 Corinthians, we recall Paul's statement about the "gospel of the glory of Christ, who is the image [*eikōn*] of God" (4:4) and the long sentence a few lines earlier:

> And all of us, with unveiled faces, seeing as in a mirror the glory of the Lord, are being transformed into the same image from one degree of glory to another; for this comes from the Lord, the Spirit. (2 Cor 3:18)

In light of these sentences from 2 Corinthians, it is clear that the "hope of sharing the glory of God" in Romans 5:2 refers to arriving at the fullness of transformation into the likeness to God displayed in the risen Christ.

For the present, such full conformity to the resurrection of Christ remains a matter of hope. It represents what Paul terms "salvation." Meanwhile, we are simply "on the way," living in an "in-between" time: between "justification" (which is behind us) and "salvation" (which lies ahead).

Although it may be hard for us to grasp, the conditions of this "in-between time" presented a considerable problem for the early generations of believers, Paul included. Unlike fellow Jews who had not come to faith in Christ, they were maintaining that Jesus of Nazareth was Israel's long-awaited Messiah. All very well for them, but Jews who had not come to faith might well retort, "You say he's the Messiah. Well, the times don't look very 'messianic'! Look out the window. Same old world. Not much evidence that all those prophecies of Isaiah and so forth about the Messianic Age have been fulfilled."

Maintaining belief in Jesus as the Messiah meant confronting such challenges. It meant facing two features of the present situation in particular: suffering and the continuing prevalence of death. A further issue to be addressed concerned the necessity and possibility of living righteously in this in-between time: how to live out the new status of right relationship with God, without going back to the practice of the Jewish law; what is the basis for living righteously in this time of grace when one is on the way to salvation but has not yet arrived?

These are the issues that dominate Paul's argument for hope across Romans 5—8. He begins by addressing the experience of suffering in the first half of chapter 5 (vv. 1–11). He comes back to it in the second half of chapter 8 (vv. 17–39). Let us for the present focus on the first half of Romans 5.

As we are all too aware, when a person, especially a devoutly religious person, is confronted with suffering, there is a strong temptation to think that they are being punished by God, punished perhaps for some sin of the past, even for one they have forgotten. In Paul's situation, suffering, especially in the shape of persecution, could lead believers to feel that they are still under the wrath of God, that they are not destined for salvation as they are, and that perhaps they should go back to the practice of the Law in order to satisfy the divine demands and so escape the wrath. Understood in this way, suffering would pose a strong challenge to the hope of salvation that is the main theme of the entire section (Romans 5—8). So Paul interprets suffering in a totally new key. Defiantly, in fact, he begins by asserting that "we boast in our sufferings" and then sets out a steplike sequence of rather stoic tenor:

> And not only that, but we also boast in our *sufferings*,
> knowing that *suffering* produces *endurance*,
> and *endurance* produces *character*,
> and *character* produces *hope*. (Rom 5:3–4)

It is not certain that what Paul asserts so confidently here is always the case. Rather than producing endurance and character and ultimately hope, suffering may often give rise to distress and despair. We don't have to agree with Paul on everything.

He surely does much better when he continues:

> and hope does not disappoint us, because God's love has been poured into our hearts through the Holy Spirit that has been given to us. (v. 5)

In the face of suffering, the Spirit, imaged here as "water poured out into our hearts," communicates a sense, not of God's wrath, but of God's love: not our love for God, but God's love for us. Here, the Spirit functions in Paul's view as the felt experience of God's love. Hope flows from this sense of being loved by God communicated by the Spirit into the depths of our hearts. On one level, Paul may have in mind here a more overtly charismatic experience of the Spirit such as the gift of tongues. It is also possible to find here a reference to the more intimate touch of the Spirit that St. Ignatius dubs "consolation," when the soul is "inflamed with the love of its Creator and Lord," rendered "quiet and tranquil," full of "interior joy" ("Rules for the Discernment of Spirits," *Spiritual Exercises*, §318).

The remaining sentences of the passage (vv. 6–10) reinforce the case for hope stemming from this awareness of God's love communicated by the Spirit. Paul uses an a priori argument to which he often has recourse, especially in Romans. The argument comes in two "waves," in which Paul reasons from the extremity of love that God has *already* shown in the sending and death of the Son, to the certainty that God will see us through to full salvation. So the first "wave" runs as follows:

> For while we were still weak, at the right time Christ died for the ungodly. Now, rarely will any- one die for a righteous person—though perhaps for

a good person someone might actually dare to die. But what proves God's love for us in that while we still were sinners Christ died for us. Much more surely then, now that we have been justified by his blood, will we be saved through him from the wrath. (vv. 6–9)

One of the topics for discussion among educated writers in the Greco-Roman world was friendship and, more specifically, the question, "For what kind of person or friend might one be prepared to give up one's life?" Paul records one response: though such preparedness to die for another would be very rare, it might be appropriate in the case of a really good person (v. 7). What is unthinkable, however, is that one would die for an unworthy person, for a sinner. Yet that is exactly what Christ did: he entered into a world alienated from God and gave his life for us sinners (v. 8). So Paul's conclusion, on an a fortiori basis, runs, "If, while we were in this situation of alienation ['enemies!'], God displayed such love by sending his Son to die for us, how much more can we be certain that, now that we are in right relationship with him, indeed loved by him [attested by the gift of the Spirit], will God see us through to full salvation" (v. 9).

Many translations add the phrase "of God" after "wrath" at the end of verse 9 (e.g., NRSV; NIV; JB ["God's anger"]). They are trying perhaps to be helpful by specifying that the reference is to divine wrath, but there is nothing corresponding to that phrase in the Greek original (so, rightly, NAB). The addition is not helpful at all. In this context, where Paul is emphasizing God's love, why make explicit a reference to God's wrath that is not actually there? In a remote way, yes, wrath is a reference to divine anger, but only in an objective biblical sense where it designates not so much an emotion in God but the state of permanent separation or standoff from God that is the antithesis of salvation.

The second "wave" of the argument offers a more succinct version of the same a fortiori logic:

> For if while we were enemies, we were reconciled
> to God through the death of his Son, much more
> surely, having been reconciled, will we be saved by
> his life. (v. 10)

Here, as in 2 Corinthians 5:18–19, the motif of "reconciliation" emerges explicitly with respect to the divine act of redemption. Prior to that act, "we" (that is, the human race) were in a situation of "enmity" to God. It was into this situation of hostility that God in the person of the Son made a costly entry in order to effect reconciliation and "peace" (see v. 1). If God went to such an extremity of love in the "harder" case (toward "enemies"), how much more certain can we be that the same divine love will see us through to full salvation in the "easier" case (now that we are reconciled and at peace).

REFLECTION

One thing that emerges from this argument is the absolute continuity between the love of God the Father and the love of the Son. In his becoming incarnate and in his entire human life up to his "obedient" death on the cross (Phil 2:8), the Son is entirely the embodiment of God's love, the divine love that has reached out to us in our alienation and that is now accompanying us "on the way" to the fullness of salvation. In Paul's view, our lives are being carried along on this great wave of divine love. That is the fundamental basis for hope. Suffering is in no way to be interpreted as a sign of divine disfavor. On the contrary, as Paul more explicitly indicates when he returns to the theme in chapter 8 of Romans (v. 17), suffering is a sign of deeper union with Christ, in particular, union with him in his redemptive suffering for the life of the world.

SUGGESTED SCRIPTURE

Romans 4:13–25; 5:1–11; 2 Corinthians 3:18—4:6; Galatians 4:1–7; 1 Peter 1:3–9; 2:4–10; Psalms 39 (40); 102 (103); Isaiah 51:9–16; 52:1–10; 54:4–10; 56:3–8; 62:1–5

PERSONAL REFLECTION

How does this passage bear upon my "operative" image of God: that is, the image of God that governs my prayer, my attitudes, and my activity?

Where do I experience the touch of the Spirit ("consolation") in my heart? What seems to lead to this? What effect does it have on my daily life?

What gives me hope? Where, on the contrary, do I find myself falling away from hope? What leads to this?

Are there aspects of my life where I am still at "enmity" with God? Are there places within me where I need to invite, with confidence, the divine reconciling presence?

How do I relate the experience of suffering to my life with God?

THE OLD ADAM AND THE NEW

We have already considered Paul's view of Christ as "New Adam" in connection with the Christ-hymn in Philippians 2:6–11. There the allusion to Adam is implicit rather than expressly stated. In Romans 5:12–21, however, continuing the case for hope from the previous section (5:1–11), Paul sets up a sustained comparison between Adam and Christ. This portrayal of Christ in Adamic terms emerges from the comparison to become a significant motif in the letter, with much to contribute, I believe, to a spirituality derived from St. Paul. Let us now consider the passage in some detail, before spending time with the following passage (6:1–13), where, in a more ethical vein, Paul provides a basis for Christian living in an epoch of grace.

THE OLD ADAM AND THE NEW (ROM 5:12–21)

In the second half of Romans 5, Paul addresses the second of the two great issues that confront believers in the "in-between" time in which they currently live. There is a shift, that is, from the problem of suffering to that of death. If, as asserted in 5:1–11, suffering cannot erode Christian hope, so neither can death. Despite the prevalence of death in the human race, a hope of salvation remains because the forces of sin leading to death are no match for the power of divine grace leading to (eternal) life in Christ Jesus.

To assert this truth, Paul draws on a Jewish tradition about Adam as the instigator of sin and death and juxtaposes him against Christ as instrument of grace leading to righteousness and life. Adam is at once the representative and determinant of humanity gone wrong; Christ, as "Last [that is, latter-day] Adam" (1 Cor 15:45) is the representative and facilitator of humanity going right—going, that is, in accordance with the original and still valid design of the Creator. "In Adam," to use Paul's language, is told the "sin" and "death" story of the human race; "in Christ" is told the "righteousness" and "life" story of the human race. These two "stories" lay a claim on every human life. We "inhabit" each story as long as we live. And, as already noted, this sense of human life being under the tug, so to speak, of two opposing spiritual forces, is one area where Paul's understanding and that of Ignatius largely cohere, albeit couched in different language.

One essential thing to grasp is that, in Paul's view, the two stories do not have equal weight. The reason there is hope that life rather than death will win out is that the story told in Christ is so much more powerful than the one told in Adam. This must be so because, whereas Adam represents simply a sinful human being (albeit one representative of the entire race), behind Christ stands the love and grace of God. Only a pessimistic theology would see the corruption of human nature as a match for divine grace.

Unfortunately, in the sustained comparison between Adam and Christ that he sets up in this passage, Paul doesn't get his case for hope off to a helpful start. Over and over again in the passage, he sets up the contrast between the two figures and their respective legacies, emphasizing in each case the superiority of grace. At the very start, however, finishing the negative, "Adam" side (v. 12), he breaks off to make an explanatory aside (vv. 13–14) and fails to complete the positive balancing assurance about Christ. He begins as follows:

> Therefore, just as sin came into the world through
> one man, and through sin [came] death, and

so death spread to all on the basis that all have sinned... (v. 12)

He then should have carried on with a positive counter-statement, such as the following:

just so, righteousness came into the world through one man, and through righteousness life, so that life might spread to all on the basis of receiving righteousness as a gift through faith.

Instead, he breaks off to formulate an explanation about the onset of death in the absence of law (vv. 13–14). The explanation is something we would relegate to a footnote and need not concern us further here.

However, the upshot was that the Christian theological tradition, led especially by Augustine, got hooked on that first negative clause and its assertion of a nexus between sin deriving from Adam and the onset of death in the human race. This connection became the primary focus of attention in the Western theological tradition, thereby ensuring that the text was seen to be all about sin and death rather than about the overwhelming superiority of grace, leading to righteousness and life.

Actually, Paul seems to get nervous about the comparison he's drawing between Adam and Christ. He begins very soon (v. 15) to stress over and over the contrast rather than the likeness between them. They are similar in one way and one way only: that each has an effect on the entire human race. In every other way, however, they are different: in the circumstances they had to deal with and, above all, in the effects they brought: sin and death in the one case, righteousness and life in the other.[3]

It is this "unlikeness" that Paul seems to be stressing in verses 15–17, although the language is cryptic and the allusions too intricate to explore in detail. Note, however, the strength of the affirmations of God's grace on the positive side:

> If through one man's trespass many died, *much more* have the grace of God and the gift in the grace of the one man Jesus Christ abounded for many. (v. 15)

And then verse 17 (one of my favorite sentences in Paul!):

> For if through one man's trespass, death reigned through that one man, *much more* will those who accept the overflow of grace and gift of righteousness reign in life through the one man Jesus Christ.

Notice the reiterated "much more," Paul's a fortiori logic coming out again. Note also, the absolute continuity between God's grace and Christ's "gift in grace," that is, the giving up of his life for all. Christ is the embodiment of divine grace, the *charisma* of God.[4]

Without going into detail, let us note the explicit contrast in verse 19 between the "disobedience" of "one man" (Adam) and its effects, on the one hand, and the "obedience" of Christ, and its effects, on the other:

> As through one man's disobedience many were made sinners, so through one man's obedience many will be made righteous.

We are back with the thought the Philippians hymn (2:6–11). Christ's obedience ("unto death" [Phil 2:8]) was obedience to his "likeness" ("equality" [2:6]) to God, displayed in laying down his life in self-emptying love. In taking on the sin-burden of the human race and submitting to death on that account, he countered the Adamic legacy of sin and death, and opened the way for all to share his own risen life. As a consequence, all can make their own Paul's reference to "the Son of God, who loved me and delivered himself up for me" (Gal 2:20).

To bring out the hope that flows from the overwhelming power of grace, Paul concludes,

> Where sin increased, grace abounded all the more [literally, "super-abounded"]. So that as sin reigned in death, grace also might reign through righteousness, leading to eternal life, through Jesus Christ, our Lord. (vv. 20b–21)

There are, of course, aspects of Paul's reclamation of the "Adam" myth that present difficulty for interpretation today. From what we know scientifically about human origins and especially from a contemporary sense of justice, we cannot be at ease with a sense of legacy of sin, let alone guilt, deriving from a single, representative ancestor. Nor do we see physical death as a punishment for sin but rather as a natural aspect of the human condition. We have also previously noted that the classical doctrine of "Original Sin" as affirmed by the Council of Trent—largely following Augustine's reading of this Pauline passage—stands sorely in need of fresh theological formulation.

Nonetheless, what emerges helpfully from Paul's Adam/Christ contrast far outweighs the liabilities. What emerges, above all, is that human life is not lived on neutral terrain. Two forces tug on each human life: a force drawing toward sin and death, on the one hand, and a force (divine grace) leading to life. In these central chapters of Romans (5—8), Paul personifies these forces (Sin, Death, Grace, Righteousness, Life, etc.), making them like actors in a medieval mystery play. He portrays Sin (*hamartia*) as a tyrant power under whose enslaving grip Adam has brought the human race. Correspondingly, he represents Grace, embodied in Christ, as a liberating—and more powerful—force for life. The personification lends a mythological tone to the argument, but Paul is not suggesting that human beings have become helpless tools of powers "outside" of themselves. For Paul, sin represents the tyranny of radical selfishness, the deadly virus that ruins relationships in all directions: with God, with our fellow human beings, with one's body, and the wider environment. Without denying individual responsibility, Paul appeals to the Adam myth as a symbol of this collective solidarity in sin. No one sins entirely alone and no one sins without adding to the sin burden of the race. But just as Adam "models" human relating selfishly and destructively in all directions, the "New" or "Last Adam" (Christ) models—and facilitates—human relating in a totally unselfish and constructive way (Phil 2:6–8; Rom 15:3). Appealing to the figure of Adam, Paul presents a human solidarity in sin and death, but only as a foil to a "much more" powerful solidarity in grace and life that God has brought about in Christ. It is the prevailing power of this new solidarity that gives rise to hope.

We will come across more of this hope when we consider a further trace of the Adam story in Romans 8. For the present, Paul's "Adam" Christology is attractive primarily in its implication that the salvation that Christ has brought and continues to bring to the human race is not a kind of supernatural "icing" on the "cake" of human nature. Rather, it has to do with humanity as such. It is about human beings becoming truly human as the Creator intended us to be. As stated so aptly in Ephesians, it involves our "growing up" to the full "adult" stature of Christ (4:13).

CHRISTIAN LIVING IN AN EPOCH OF GRACE (ROM 6:1–13)

The emphasis that Paul places on the overwhelming power of grace is fine, but it can lead and evidently did lead in his time to people saying, "Well, why, then, be righteous?

Why not continue in sin, seeing that it will not attract condemnation but provide even greater scope for God's grace?" Paul lets an objection along these lines rise at the beginning of chapter 6 and scotches it immediately (v. 1). It does, however, seem to represent one that he had to face from rivals and critics in the Christian mission (see Rom 3:8), especially those who were worried about not requiring Gentile converts to adopt a life of obedience to the Law. What else could constrain them to live righteously in the face of such an emphasis on grace?

In the passage that follows, Paul provides a basis for righteous living in an era of grace, that is, in the "in-between" time in which believers find themselves, the time when we have to live out the new—and indeed final—relationship with God while still anchored, bodily at least, in the conditions of the old era, where suffering, physical death, and temptation remain. This is the essential challenge of Pauline spirituality: how to live as "citizens" of the new creation that has dawned in Christ, when, as far as our bodily existence is concerned, the conditions of the old creation still prevail. In other words, how to live out the "grace" story told in Christ, while the "Adam" story has yet to run its full course (see 1 Cor 15:20–28). Paul tackles this issue in Romans 6:1–13.

In regard to this passage, it is important to keep in mind that, as we have noted already, for literary and rhetorical effect, Paul is personifying forces that really are aspects of human behavior on the one hand or divine action on the other. Here, it is clear that he pictures Sin—in effect radical selfishness—as a tyrannical slave master whose commands and edicts, aside from the influence of Grace, human beings must obey.

The most radical way of being set free from slavery is to die. Drastic, yes, but effective! Paul reminds his audience in Romans 6 that their baptism has meant an entry *into* Christ that was not just an entry into his person in a static way but an entry also into the dynamic of his entire "career": his death, burial, and resurrection:

> Do you not know that all of us who have been baptized into Christ Jesus were baptized into his death? Therefore we have been buried with him by baptism into death, so that, just as Christ was raised from the dead by the glory of the Father, so we too might walk in newness of life. For if we have been united with him in a death like his, we will certainly be united with him in a resurrection like his. We know that our old self was crucified with him to take away the body of sin, so that we might no longer be enslaved to sin. For whoever has died is freed from sin. But if we have died with Christ, we believe that we will also live with him. We know that Christ, being raised from the dead, will never die again; death no longer has dominion over him. The death he died, he died to sin, once for all; but the life he lives, he lives to God. So you also must consider yourselves dead to sin and alive to God in Christ Jesus. (6:3–11)

Over and over again, in his wave-like pattern of argument, Paul reaffirms our baptismal participation in the death of Christ. Having died in this sacramental sense, we are free from the claims of the tyrannical slave master, Sin. We no longer *have* to obey its death-dealing commands.

Of course, Paul knows that sin remains a problem in Christian communities. Here, he is not so much asserting the "impossibility" of postbaptismal sin but rather its total inappropriateness in the new era of grace.[5] The new life "in Christ" inaugurated in baptism means that Christ, as risen Lord, lays claim on the bodies of believers in order to continue to live out his self-sacrificial love in their bodily life. As he lived and continues to live "for God," that is, in total, loving obedience to the Father (vv. 9–10), so believers should consider themselves "dead" as far as the claims of Sin are concerned and similarly "alive to God" through their existence "in Christ" (v. 11).

The sequence concludes with a little exhortation on life in the body:

> Let not sin therefore reign in your mortal body, to make you obey its desires. And do not offer your members to sin as instruments of wickedness, but, instead, offer yourselves to God as people brought back to life from the dead, and your members as instruments of righteousness to God. (vv. 12–13)

We can recognize here Paul's sophisticated sense of "body" (*sōma* in Greek). Paul thinks of the body above all as the instrument of communication: communication between the self and the world of persons and things outside the self, to give and receive impressions. "Body" refers to more than just the material aspect of the human person. It denotes the whole person particularly under the aspect of this capacity for communication and relationship. When Paul speaks more specifically of "members" (*melē*) in this short passage, he is probably thinking not so much of the extremities of the body, such as hands and feet, but of the whole complex of ways in which human beings relate objectively to the world of persons and things outside the self. The Greek word translated as "instruments" (*hopla*) also serves to render "weapons"—the instruments with which a soldier wages war—likewise a fisherman's tackle or a carpenter's tools.

REFLECTION

Paul's urging his audience to offer their whole bodily life in this dynamic sense to the service of "righteousness" is particularly rich when we recall the meaning this term has for him. All true righteousness is ultimately the righteousness or saving fidelity of God, embodied in the world in the person and mission of Christ. We recall the striking statement concerning the purpose of his mission at the end of 2 Corinthians 5:

> God made him who knew no sin into sin, so that
> in him we might become the righteousness of God.
> (v. 21)

Not, "that we might become righteous" but "that we might become the righteousness of God." In other words, as Christ embodies God's saving faithfulness (righteousness) to the world, so Christians, baptized "into Christ," are by the same token baptized into that same saving faithfulness, becoming instruments thereby of the divine offer to the world of reconciliation and life.

Thus, Paul would argue that his strong emphasis on God's grace in passages such as Romans 5:12–21 in no way undercuts the need for believers to live a righteous life. On the contrary, living within the "grace" story told in Christ rather than the "sin" story told in Adam means living in the world as Christ lived in the world and wishes to continue to live out his loving obedience to the Father in our bodily life. Surely there is a strong basis for Christian ethics and spirituality here.

SUGGESTED SCRIPTURE

Romans 5:12–21; 6:1–14; 13:8–14; Galatians 5:1–6; Ephesians 4:11–16; Philippians 1:3–11; Colossians 3:12–17; 1 Thessalonians 5:1–11

PERSONAL REFLECTION

How does Paul's presentation of Christ as "New" or "Last Adam" affect my image of Christ and my understanding of what he brings to the world?

Are there areas in my life where the "Adam" story rather than the "Christ" story prevail?

How might Christ live out his continuing obedience to the Father in my bodily life?

How am I drawn more deeply into the saving faithfulness (righteousness) of God toward the world?

DAY 6

FROM CAPTIVITY TO
FREEDOM IN THE SPIRIT

We have already noted Paul's understanding of the Spirit as the felt or palpable experience of God's love (Rom 5:5). As such, the Spirit is the guarantee that justification, right relationship with God, is behind us. We are right with God, living the relationship with God that goes with the new creation that has already dawned in Christ, even if aspects of the old era—suffering, temptation, and physical death—remain. The Spirit is a divine pledge of hope because it assures believers that none of these forces should distance us from God's love. As mentioned already, the experience of the Spirit in this sense corresponds to the Ignatian sense of "consolation," the experience that, carefully discerned, assures people that they are in line with the way God is drawing them into life.

Now we are to consider a further role of the Spirit, namely, as the power that enables us, in this "in-between" time, to live out the right relationship with God, and so remain on track to salvation. In Pauline terms, this means living "according to the Spirit" rather than "according to the flesh."

FLESH, LAW, AND SPIRIT

First, a word in passing on "flesh" (*sarx*) in Paul. It is one of the most difficult terms to translate. The *Jerusalem Bible* renders it "our unspiritual nature," which just begs the question because it leaves open what "spiritual" means. The main thing in regard to "flesh" is not to identify it totally with our physical, bodily existence. "Flesh" can simply refer to the physical body, but Paul more regularly uses "flesh" in the biblical sense of human existence in its fragility, weakness, and proneness to sin over against God, whereas "spirit" (with a small "s") refers to human existence in its capacity to relate positively to God. God's Holy Spirit calls the human spirit to life. In line with this biblical usage, "flesh" for Paul refers to human existence in its proneness to self-absorption, selfishness and sin. It is not exactly identical to sin; it is the base that sin can exploit in human life. Thus, "sins of the flesh" do not necessarily refer in Paul to wrong sexual behavior. Sins such as backbiting, gossip, lying, which have nothing to do with sex, are equally manifestations of the "flesh"—and perhaps more destructively so than overtly bodily vices such as gluttony or sexual sin. Thus, to "live according to the flesh" for Paul is basically to live selfishly and destructively in regard to relations with others and especially with God.

It is impossible when giving an account of Paul's theology or spirituality to avoid mention of the most neuralgic topic in his thought: that of the Law. The issue is difficult for us since we are not exercised by the Law of Moses or tempted to adopt it. Paul's preoccupation with the Law had to do with the attempt by rival Christian missionaries to impose its practice—what he refers to as "works of the law"—on converts from the non-Jewish, Gentile world. That is not our concern, and largely due to the efforts of Paul, it has not been the concern of Christians for centuries. However, his analysis of why the Law wouldn't work and shouldn't be imposed on new converts retains considerable resonance in our lives today. More specifically, his depiction of life under the Law and the liberating transition from that condition to life in the Spirit remains as relevant today as it did when he wrote to the community in Rome nearly two millennia ago.

Paul sets out this transition across the final section of Romans 7 and the first section of Romans 8. These two passages (7:14–25 and 8:1–13) should always be held together. The chapter division coming between them—though understandable—is unfortunate in this respect. The powerful force of Paul's rhetoric here is undercut if we do not see how he holds them up in contrastive parallel—like a diptych painting in religious art.

LIFE UNDER THE LAW (ROM 7:14–25)

The struggle depicted in 7:14–25 is one of the most powerful passages in Paul and one that has readily arrested the attention of people down the ages. In three, largely parallel "waves" a speaker ("I") laments the moral captivity in which it finds itself, unable, despite its best intentions, to obey the Law, because the indwelling power of Sin—still personified—is calling the shots. It will suffice to quote here simply the first of these rhetorical "waves":

> The law, as we know, is spiritual. But I am fleshly, sold into slavery under sin. I am completely at a loss to account for my own behavior. For it is not what I want to do that I do. But I do what I hate. If what I do is contrary to my will, this means that I agree with the law and hold it to be admirable. But the situation is that it is no longer I who do this but sin dwelling within me. (7:14–17)

Two questions immediately arise in connection with this passage. The first has to do with the identity of the "I" who speaks here. The most natural interpretation is to hear Paul speaking autobiographically and describing his own struggles under the yoke of the Law. However, there is no suggestion anywhere else in Paul's letters that the practice of the Law was a struggle for him. In Philippians 3:5, he claims to have been "perfect" in regard to righteousness, that is, practice of the Law. In his letters, for purposes of rhetorical effect, he occasionally lapses into the first person singular when speaking representatively, that is, speaking in a way that applies to members of a group in a particular situation (see, for example, Gal 2:18–21). That is also likely to be the case here.

But now we run into the second question. What is the situation of the group for whom the "I" is speaking? Is the "I" speaking as a believer, describing the struggle that believers continue to have even in the new life in Christ? That has been a venerable interpretation in the Christian tradition. It has the merit and indeed the attractiveness of resonating very much with the way we often feel when presented with duty or moral demand. As the Roman poet Ovid expressed memorably so long ago, *Video meliora proboque; deteriora sequor* ("I see the better way and I approve it; but I follow the worse").[1] The fact that Paul writes in the present tense also suggests that he has present Christian life in view.

Against this, however, is the unambiguous complaint of the "I" at the start of the passage about being "sold into slavery under sin" (v. 14). That situation of slavery should be a thing of the past for the believer. It is directly contrary to the sense of having "died" to sin that Paul has insisted on over and over in the preceding passages (Rom 6:6–11, 14, 17–18; 7:5–6). It is far more likely that Paul is attempting to depict graphically the situation of a person confronted with the demands of the Law of Moses—or any law—before coming under the liberation brought by Christ. The problem with the Law is that it remains purely external to human beings. It addresses a series of "do's" and "don'ts," mainly the latter, to a person still very much living "in the flesh," that is, living under the domination of the flesh. As such, like the command given to Adam, rather than helping foster compliance with what it commands, it actually provokes rebellion. It makes matters worse, intensifying rather than suppressing the regime of the tyrant slave master, Sin, in the flesh.

The passage dramatically depicts this grim scenario in three waves of frustrated lament (vv. 15–17, 18–20, 21–23), before building to a great climax with the "I" exclaiming, "Wretched one that I am! Who will deliver me from the body of this death?" (v. 24). A first answer is then given, "Thanks be to God through Jesus Christ, our Lord" (v. 25a). However, these words are more likely a very early addition to the manuscript tradition rather than a response written by Paul himself.[2]

REDEEMED BY GOD'S ACT IN CHRIST (ROM 8:1–4)

Paul's own response to the desperate cry of the "I" comes in the second "panel" of the diptych as we break into chapter 8, with its ringing theme:

There is now no condemnation for those in Christ Jesus. For the law of the Spirit of life has set you free from the law of sin and death. (8:1–2)

The run of phrases in the second verse should be understood adjectivally: the law that consists of the life-giving Spirit has set you free from the "law" (that is, the regime) of Sin leading to death. The true solution to the ethical plight of the "I," the reason that the threat of "condemnation" (at the judgment) has been lifted (v. 1), is that "in Christ," that is, in the new existence brought about by God's redemptive act, the Spirit has replaced the regime of Sin as indwelling, determining power.

A long statement of God's act explains how this has come about:

> For what the law could not do, in that it was weak because of the flesh, God [has done]: sending his Son in the likeness of flesh dominated by sin, and to deal with sin, he condemned sin in the flesh, in order that the righteous requirement of the law might be fulfilled in us, who walk now, not according to the flesh, but according to the Spirit. (vv. 3–4)

The first clause sums up the problem: the impotence of the Law to do anything to help. The Law could not help—but in fact only made things worse—because it stood outside the "I," making moral demands but unable to address the root problem which lay within the person: the regime of Sin in the "flesh."

In the face of this impotence of the Law, God has acted, sending the Son to deal with the problem at its radical core. Where the Law remained external and impotent on that account, the Son came "in the likeness of sinful flesh." As in 2 Corinthians 5:21 ("God made him who knew no sin, into sin"), Paul does not hesitate to stress the radicality of the Son's entrance into the sinful human situation (as in the Philippians hymn as well: "taking the form of a slave and becoming as humans are" [Phil 2:7]). There, personally bearing (on the cross) the cost of that entry, Christ dealt with Sin right there where Sin had been dominant, so that the "condemnation" that would have fallen on human beings (v. 1) falls instead on the real villain: "sin in the flesh."

We should note here in passing how closely Paul's sense of Christ entering into the depths of human sinfulness in order to release the Spirit and heal it from within conforms to the characteristic behavior of Jesus Christ as described in the Gospels, especially his notorious and ultimately costly preference for associating with "sinners" and outcasts, rather than with the righteous (see, e.g., Luke 5:27–32 [Matt 9:9–13; Mark 2:13–17]; 15:1–2).

The upshot of Christ's redemptive entrance into the human situation is that the righteousness that the Law required but could not bring about "is fulfilled in us," who live now (literally, "who walk now"), not according to the flesh but according to the Spirit (v. 4). Notice the passive formulation: not that "we might fulfill" but "might be fulfilled in us." The passive indicates the action of God and communicates the sense that the new capacity to live righteously, while it is "ours" because expressed in our bodily life, is fundamentally the achievement of God's Spirit within us. The passive construction wards off any sense of "earning" God's favor. It is all fundamentally the effect of divine grace.[3]

We may also note once again the "trinitarian" shape of this rich theological statement in verses 3 and 4. God the Father sends the Son to release in human beings the empowering Spirit, enabling them to live righteously in the new era of grace. The ethical life of believers, our capacity to live out the gift of righteousness, is entirely the product of the triune God. It is the "embodiment" in human living of the "righteousness of God" that, in the person of the Son, represents the faithfulness of the Creator to the world. Through faith and baptism "into Christ" we are built into God's fidelity to the world, Christ's faithful "obedience" in this respect (2 Cor 5:21; Rom 6:13).

If the preceding power calling the shots in human life was that of sin, that is, radical selfishness, the new determining power is the exact opposite: the self-sacrificial love of God in the shape of the Spirit. The Spirit becomes the true antidote to sin, the love of God that turns back and wipes away the whole human tide of sin. In the face of human sin, the Law could only condemn from outside. Christ made a costly entrance into the depth of the human situation and addressed the problem at its core.

Paul has insisted, of course, that in itself the Law is "just and holy and good" (7:12). The values it enshrines, especially in the Ten Commandments (Exod 20:1–17; Deut 5:1–21), are the core values for leading a righteous life. The problem was that it couldn't get those values effectively into the human heart so that the "I" would *be able* to live according to them. The entry of Christ into the depths of the human condition and the release of the Spirit has achieved what the Law, being purely external, could not do.

Paul did not regard this replacement of the Mosaic Law by the Spirit as the disruption of the heritage of Israel. On the contrary, as allusions in some texts (see 2 Cor 3:6; Rom 2:29) show, he saw it as the fulfillment of a divine promise concerning the Messianic Age contained in the prophetic record: notably the pledge in Jeremiah to place the Law "within" the people (31:33), paralleled in Ezekiel 36:26–27 in terms of placing within them a "new spirit" (that is, the Holy Spirit).

LIVING OUT THE FREEDOM CREATED BY THE SPIRIT (ROM 8:5–11)

The following passage (8:5–11) spells out what is involved in living out this new capacity gifted by the indwelling Spirit.

> For those who live according to the flesh have their minds set on the things of the flesh, while those who live according to the Spirit have their minds set on the things of the Spirit. Now the mind-set of the flesh leads to death, whereas the mind-set of the Spirit leads to life and peace. This is because the mind-set of the flesh is hostility to God. For it is not subject to the law of God, nor can it be.... But you are not living in the power of the flesh but in that of the Spirit—if the Spirit of God is indeed dwelling in you....But if Christ dwells in you, then, while the body may be mortal because of sin, the Spirit means life because of righteousness. If the Spirit of the One who raised Jesus from the dead dwells in you, then the One who raised Christ from the dead will make alive also your mortal bodies through the power of his Spirit dwelling in you. (8:5–11)

Here, we see Paul glancing back for a while (vv. 5–8) at the negative. He contrasts living "according to the flesh" with the new capacity to live "according to the Spirit." There remains a degree of tension within present Christian life. It is still *possible* to live according to the flesh, with the "hostility" to God that characterized the old era prior to reconciliation (2 Cor 5:18–20; Rom 5:10–11) and the destiny to (eternal) death to which it leads. It is still possible to live in that way, but crucially and in stark contrast to the preceding situation under the Law (7:14–25), it is not *necessary* to do so. The powerful grip of the "slave master" (sin) has been broken. What had been a fatal tension, tearing the "I" apart (7:14–25), has become a constructive tension, impelling believers constantly to grow within the new freedom created in them by the Spirit, in life and "peace" with God (v. 6b).

Here, we must keep in mind Paul's biblical understanding of "flesh" (*sarx*) as referring not simply to human sensuality ("sins of the flesh") but to a whole pattern of life that is self-absorbed, selfish, and hostile to God. Clearly contrary to the flesh in this sense is the impact of the Spirit, because the Spirit is nothing other than the ongoing impact of the unselfish love of Christ. When believers live "according to the Spirit," they are allowing Christ to live out in their bodily life the divine love that led him to give himself up for us all (Rom 5:6–10; 8:3; Gal 2:20). The new "obedience" required of the Christian is nothing less than allowing the "New Adam" as "life-giving Spirit" (1 Cor 15:45) to live out his continuing "obedience" to the Father in our present life in the body. Just as the Father responded to the obedience of Christ by raising him from the dead and exalting him as "Lord" of the universe (Phil 2:9–11), so God will faithfully respond to the righteous pattern of life created by the Spirit within believers by raising also our mortal bodies to share his risen life (Rom 8:10–11).

REFLECTION

A final word about the earlier passage—the "I's" dramatic description of its plight under the Law (7:14–25): Does the interpretation of this passage as referring not to the Christian life but to life under the Law prior to becoming a believer mean that it no longer has any spiritual relevance for us as believers? This would seem contrary to experience because, for many people, it resonates with their experience in many areas of life. It does indeed continue to have relevance as a test of spirits. When we feel that this passage rather than the one that follows (8:5–11) sums up our situation—confronted by moral demands that we know we should fulfill but lacking the capacity to do so—when, like the "I" in 7:14–25, we feel torn in two by the tension and conflict, then that is probably a sign that we have, to some extent, turned away from Christ; that we have lapsed back into trying to go it alone, facing law simply as law, impinging upon us from outside. Realizing this, we can turn back to Christ and ask that he repeat his redemptive entrance into the depth of our weakness and release within us the Spirit of his love. The tension may remain, as set out in 8:5–11, but hopefully it will be a creative tension, leading to life.

SUGGESTED SCRIPTURE

Romans 7:14–25; 8:1–11; 13:8–14; Galatians 5:13–26; Jeremiah 31:31–34; Ezekiel 36:22–28; Psalm 39 (40)

PERSONAL REFLECTION

To what extent do I find myself resonating with the cry of the "I" who speaks in Romans 7:14–25? How do I interpret this in my present spiritual state?

What aspects of my character and life might correspond to Paul's understanding of "flesh"?

How do I experience the Spirit as a source of freedom in my life?

Does the claim of the gospel create in me a tension that is destructive or one that, while challenging, is also fostering of spiritual growth?

A NEW CREATION

Although Paul comes close to a systematic exposition of the gospel in Romans,[4] we have to "construct" his theology from the hints and allusions he makes when dealing with the pastoral issues that occasioned his letters. This means that some themes and motifs that appear only briefly and in passing probably bulked far more significantly in his understanding than fleeting appearances in the letters might suggest. This is probably the case with Paul's belief that what God was doing in Christ was ushering in the "new creation" (*kainē ktisis* [2 Cor 5:17; Gal 6:15]), closely linked with which was the understanding of Christ as "New" or "Last Adam" (Rom 5:12–21; 1 Cor 15:21–22, 45). In responding to the gospel with faith and in dying and rising with Christ in baptism, believers undergo a radical transfer from the old creation, with its alienation from God and slavery to sin, to the new creation where one "walks in newness of life" (Rom 6:4). The church, or perhaps more accurately to the understanding of "church" (*ekklēsia*) in Paul's day, the collection of churches in the cities of the Greco-Roman world are "beachheads" of the new creation. In the continuing conditions of the old era, believers are called to live out the values of the new, living "according to the Spirit," rather than, as before, "according to the flesh" (Rom 8:5–11; Gal 5:13–25).

As the creative force of the new creation, the Spirit is the guarantee that, despite the sufferings and limitations of the present "in-between" time, believers already belong to the new era that has dawned with the resurrection of Christ. Let us now pursue further Paul's case for hope in Romans 8, with particular attention to a remarkable passage (8:19–22), where a holistic sense of "creation," understood as embracing also the other-than-human created world, comes notably to the fore.

CHILDREN AND HEIRS OF GOD (ROM 8:14–17)

Paul leads up to this broader sense of creation in a small transition passage (8:14–17) that reintroduces explicitly the theme of hope in the face of the sufferings of the present "in-between" time (see Rom 5:3–5). The aspect of hope is bound up with a fresh description of believers that Paul introduces at this point: their status, attested by the Spirit, as "sons [and daughters] of God."

> For all whose lives are shaped by the Spirit of God are sons [and daughters] of God. For it is not a spirit of slavery that you have received—[something to drive you] back again to fear. But you have received a Spirit of sonship in which we cry out, "*Abba*, Father." The same very Spirit in this way bears witness along with our spirit that we are God's children. And if we are sons [and daughters], then we are heirs as well—heirs of God, co-heirs with Christ—provided we are prepared to suffer with him in order that we might be glorified with him. (8:14–17)

In calling believers "children of God," Paul is not coining a new metaphor for Christian life but applying to them a privilege accruing uniquely to Israel in the biblical tradition (see Exod 4:22–23; Deut 14:1; Isa 1:2–4; Hos 1:10; 11:1; Wis 18:13; Rom 9:4). The privilege of being God's "sons [and daughters]" flows from Israel's election as a people enjoying a status of closeness to God shared by no other nation. The privilege marks Israel off from other nations and is more or less interchangeable with the sense of being "the people of God." In the centuries leading up to the rise of Christianity, the image acquired a distinctly eschatological tone and came to refer to the righteous Israel of the messianic age destined to "inherit" (as God's sons and daughters) all the blessings of salvation that God as "Father" had promised to confer. It is in this eschatological sense and because he is preparing to return explicitly to the theme of hope in the face of suffering (see 5:1–11) that Paul introduces the image of believers as "sons and daughters"/"children" of God. Those who "are led by the Spirit" are those who, through the power of the indwelling Spirit (8:9–10), preserve and live out the righteousness communicated to them through Christ. As such, they are here and now God's "children" destined to "inherit" eternal life (v. 14).

In the present situation, however, where suffering and the prospect of death remain, believers need assurance that they enjoy this status. It is the Spirit that supplies the guarantee. Characteristically, Paul rules out the negative first in order to stress the positive all the more. The Spirit that we have received is not one of slavery communicating an attitude of fear. On the contrary, we have received a Spirit of sonship (*huiothesia*)[5] that makes us cry out, "*Abba*, Father" (v. 15), bearing clear witness that we enjoy the status of children of God (v. 16).

In calling to mind the *Abba* cry, Paul seems to be alluding to an experience so well-known and characteristic of Christian life as to require no further explanation, even for the community at Rome that he had not founded. There are not many places in the New Testament, aside from the Gospels, where the text preserves a word in Aramaic, the language of Palestine in Jesus' day. In Paul's writings, we find only two examples: *Maranatha* ("Our Lord, come!" [1 Cor

16:22]) and *Abba*, preserved here and in a very similar context in Galatians 4:

> But when the fullness of time had come, God sent his Son, born of a woman, born under the law, in order to redeem those who were under the law, so that we might receive the status of sonship. And to show that you are children, God has sent the Spirit of his Son into our hearts, crying, "*Abba*! Father!" So you are no longer a slave but a child, and if a child then also an heir, through God. (Gal 4:4–7)

Why did the early generation of believers preserve the Aramaic address when the Greek word for "father," *patēr*, lay at hand? It seems that we have here a reminiscence of the way in which Jesus addressed God and, in fact, taught his followers to do so. The Greek *patēr* doesn't quite catch the nuance of the Aramaic *Abba*. *Abba* is the familial address of sons and daughters to the male parent. It is not as formal as "father" (which *patēr* would convey) and not as babyish as "daddy." It more or less corresponds to "dad," an address that even adult children could use. It seems that the early disciples were so struck by the intimacy of Jesus' address to God, an address, so far as we know, unparalleled in Judaism till that time, that they felt impelled to preserve the Aramaic because of the preciousness of what it conveyed. Our Eucharistic liturgy preserves a hint of that sense of wonder when at the introduction to the Lord's Prayer, there is the phrase "we *dare* to say, 'Our Father'" (*audemus dicere*). In other words, we would not make bold to pray to God in terms of such familial intimacy if the Spirit of Jesus were not impelling us to pray to the Father in the same terms as he did. In the persons of the baptized—those "in Christ"—the Son continues to express, through the Spirit, the intimacy of his relationship with the Father. Once again (see 8:3–4), we encounter Paul's sense of believers being drawn here and now into the communion of love that is the Trinity. This recaptures in the new creation the intimacy between God and human beings intended by the Creator from the start (Gen 2) but lost through mistrust and disobedience (Gen 3).

From the status of being God's "children," it is a short step to that of being God's "heirs" (v. 17). In line with a Jewish tradition that Paul is drawing on here, what the "heirs of God" can look forward to is the "inheritance of the world" that God promised to Abraham and his descendants (Rom 4:13). Stated in this way, the inheritance reclaims the Creator's original bequest to humankind in Adam (Gen 1:26–28). In short, the blessings of salvation that believers are destined to inherit amount to nothing less than the realization in Christ of the original design of the Creator for human beings and the world.

As Paul states more explicitly in Galatians, however, believers are "descendants (literally, 'seed') of Abraham," and hence "heirs," in virtue of the union with Christ forged through faith and baptism (Gal 3:16). It is as "co-heirs of Christ" they are "heirs of God. But, as we have noted, this union with Christ is not a static thing. It is an insertion into the dynamic of his "career": an insertion into his death and burial in order to share his "glorification," that is, his arrival at the fullness of humanity that has always been the design of the Creator in our regard. The suffering of believers, then, especially the persecution they endure precisely as believers, is always suffering in union with Christ.

CREATION GROANING (ROM 8:18–22)

Having reintroduced the motif of suffering in this way, Paul continues with a bold, defiant statement that states the theme of all that follows to the end of the chapter:

> For I reckon that the sufferings of the present time
> are a small price to pay for the glory that is going
> to be revealed in us. (v. 18)

To communicate this "surpassing glory" awaiting the persecuted, Paul appeals to the witness of "creation":

> For creation awaits with eager longing the rev-
> elation of the sons [and daughters] of God. For
> creation was subjected to futility—not of its own
> volition but on account of the subduer—in the
> hope that the creation itself would be set free from
> its slavery to decay in order to share the freedom
> associated with glory of the children of God. For
> we know that the entire creation has been groan-
> ing together in the pangs of childbirth right up till
> now. (vv. 19–22)

This short passage in Romans, the only place where Paul seems to take account of the other-than-human created world, has been the focus of great interest in recent years. It has featured notably in ecological interpretations of the Bible, in the construction of "ecotheology" and indeed in "ecospirituality."[6] While such interpretations are well-grounded, some details in the text and its overall pattern of reasoning repay closer examination.

We have seen Paul personify forces impinging on human existence before—the prime example being his personifica-tion of sin. Here, in a way that seems quaintly mythological, he personifies the nonhuman created world and presents it in a quasipersonal entanglement with the fate of human beings for good and for ill.

In doing so, while obviously presupposing and alluding to the accounts of Creation in Genesis 1—3, Paul is also drawing on traditions later in the Bible that see human beings and the nonhuman created world as locked in a common fate: when humans take a fall, that redounds negatively upon creation as well; the hope is, however, that when human beings are restored to right relationship with God, that will, by the same token, impact positively upon creation as well (see, e.g., Isa 11:6–9; 55:12; Ezek 34:25–31; Hos 2:18; Wis 16:24; 19:6).

Hence, the "eager longing" with which creation awaits the revelation of the sons and daughters of God" (v. 19). "Eager longing" translates a Greek word (*apokaradokia*), used elsewhere for spectators at athletic contests who complain that they can't see the finishing line because their neighbors, in their "eager longing" to see the outcome, lean forward and block the view. "Creation" is awaiting the revelation of the sons and daughters of God in the sense that the public revelation that human beings have been restored to right relationship with God will signal the restoration of the entire creation.

As he so often tends to do, Paul accounts for this expectation on the part of creation as a kind of afterthought (vv. 20 and 21). The explanation clearly alludes to the account of the fall in Genesis 3:17–19, where the earth is "cursed" as a consequence of Adam's sin and made difficult for him to till. When creation was subjected to "futility," that is, the frustration of its purpose—its "goodness," according to the first account of Creation (Gen 1)—this was not something it wanted. It was dragged down, willy-nilly, because its fate was bound up with that of the one Paul refers to as "the subduer." Most interpreters find in "the subduer" a reference to God. A minority, including myself, interprets the "subduer" as a reference to Adam, who, after all, according to Genesis 1:26–28 (also see Ps 8), was the one meant to "subdue" creation or at least take responsibility for it. Although Paul is not at his clearest in verses 20 and 21, he seems to be saying that, because creation did not fall of its own accord, nor of its own will, it has all along cherished the hope that it would one day regain freedom from its "bondage to decay" and share in the "freedom associated with the glory of the children of God," that is, freedom from death and full arrival at the likeness to God intended by the Creator from the start.

That is why, Paul explains in verse 22, creation has been "groaning together in one great act of giving birth" from the time of the fall "until now." What he seems to have in mind here is the birth of the "new creation," or more accurately, the extension to the physical world of the new creation that has already dawned in the resurrection of Christ, the impact of which believers experience through the gift of the Spirit (1 Cor 15:45).

REFLECTION

The personification of "creation" as a unity groaning in childbirth lends a highly mythological note to Romans 8:19–22. The text can hardly have a literal application to our situation today. Nonetheless, an imaginative approach does allow us to derive from it an interpretation valid for our time of ecological concern. The allusion to the "fall" narrative of Genesis 3 allows us to see an Adamic thread running here. Adam, as representative of all humanity, is "the subduer" on account of whose sin, creation was subjected to futility, to the frustration of its true purpose. As we saw in connection with Romans 5:12–21, "in Adam" is told the sin story of the human race. What this text adds is a sense of how that story impacts ruinously upon the rest of creation. It is not fanciful to see exploitative and destructive human pollution of the environment as part of that story.

However, as we also saw in Romans 5:12–21, alongside the sin story of the human race told in Adam, God has established a grace story told in Christ, who truly bears "the image and likeness" of God. If there is hope for the human race, it is because, as Paul insists over and over again (Rom 5:15–21), the grace story is "much more" powerful than the sin story because behind it and bringing it to prevalence is the power and faithfulness of God. If creation has suffered and continues to suffer from the ravages of human sin, there is hope that it may benefit when and where the grace story prevails.

In this perspective, the world is not some kind of vast playpen in which God lets us act out our lives for a time, testing us to see if we are worthy to live in some other realm. There are indeed strands in the biblical tradition that give rise to such a view. However, there would seem to emerge from this text a real continuity between the present world and the life of the world to come. Where "resurrection" seems to imply a moment at least of radical discontinuity (destruction and death, followed by re-creation in some form), what emerges here is more a sense of transformation, rather than destruction and beginning all over again.

The upshot of all this is that the future of the world is very much in human hands. This does not mean that God sits back and does nothing. God is ever-active as Creator, but human beings play a central role in the creation of a positive future for the world insofar as they allow themselves to be instruments of grace, yielding their "members" as instruments of "righteousness" to God (Rom 6:13). Hope for the future does not derive from an optimistic view of the present situation. It does not mean that if human beings ruin the world, the Creator will effect a kind of *deus ex machina* rescue. Hope springs ultimately from the fidelity of God to creation, a fidelity that through grace can prevail in the human sphere and in the wider world that is "our common home."

Many strands of ecology, led especially by the famous essay of the American historian Lyn White, have looked with a jaundiced eye on the Judeo-Christian tradition emanating from the early chapters of Genesis, which presents what they dub an overly "anthropocentric" view of the world. It can be said in response that whether anthropocentricism is something to applaud or on the contrary to deplore, it is a fact: for good or ill, human beings call the shots on planet Earth. The point, surely, is to ensure that they do so responsibly and creatively, that they adopt a "contemplative" approach to the rest of creation, one that respects the autonomy of other creatures, rather than the exploitative approach that has been so prevalent hitherto.[7] To this end, Paul's appeal to the voice of creation in Romans 8:19–22 can reprise the responsibility for the world divinely entrusted to human beings in Genesis 1:26–28 in a constructive, grace-filled way.

SUGGESTED SCRIPTURE

Romans 8:14–17; 8:18–22; Galatians 4:4–7; Psalm 8; Isaiah 11:6–9; 55:6–13; Ezekiel 34:25–31; Hosea 2:14–23; Revelation 21:1–7

PERSONAL REFLECTION

Can I allow Jesus to draw me into the intimacy of his *Abba* address to God?

What does being a "co-heir of Christ" add to or condition the sense of being "heirs of God" (Rom 8:17)?

In what ways is relation to or responsibility for the wider created world a significant part of my relationship with God?

Where does the "Adam" story continue to run in my life?

Where does the "grace" story, told in Christ, prevail in my life?

DAY 7

―――――◦◦◦∞◦◦◦―――――

CHRIST CRUCIFIED

The Power and Wisdom of God

No New Testament writer presents the death of Jesus in so confronting a way as Paul. Perhaps it was because it featured so centrally in his own conversion that it plays so prominent a part in his preaching of the gospel. The zeal that drove his brief career as a persecutor of the early followers of Jesus stemmed from his horror at their claim that a crucified man, one therefore upon whom fell the curse of the Law (Deut 27:26), was the Messiah of Israel. To overcome this obstacle and lead him to see the one crucified as indeed the Messiah and, in fact, God's Son required, in his view, nothing less than an act of creation: "It is the God who said, 'Let light shine out of darkness,' who has shone in our hearts to give the light of the knowledge of the glory of God in the face of Jesus Christ" (2 Cor 4:6).

For Paul, the divine love displayed in the cross functions as the supreme criterion of authentic Christian life. Hence, the frequency of references to Jesus' death in our considerations so far. It is, however, appropriate to consider at greater depth some of the passages where Paul treats the subject in a more sustained and intentional way.

THE PREACHING OF THE CRUCIFIED CHRIST (1 COR 1:18—2:5)

Paul, it would seem, did not avoid mention of the cross or approach it gradually. He confronted his hearers with the stark reality, relying simply on the grace of God to bring about a response in faith in the human heart. Listen to his strong language as he reminds the Galatians of his initial preaching:

> You foolish Galatians! Who has bewitched you? It was before your eyes that Jesus Christ was publicly exhibited as crucified! The only thing I want to learn from you is this: Did you receive the Spirit by doing the works of the law or by believing what you heard? (Gal 3:1–2)

"Publicly exhibited" is perhaps more accurately translated "publicly placarded," communicating the sense of a description given so vividly as to confront the hearer with the physical reality of what is being described: here, the crucifixion of Jesus. Paul is reminding the Galatians that, as in the case of his own conversion (Gal 1:16), they have been led to see the Crucified, not as a failed messianic pretender, but as God's Son, given up for the world in a supreme revelation of redemptive divine love. It was through responding in faith to that revelation that they received the Spirit and hence the assurance that they already enjoyed a status of right relationship (righteousness) with God. How futile, then, the attempt to seek righteousness through any other means, notably practice of the "works of the law"!

In a similar vein, Paul explains to the Corinthians why his initial preaching to them did not rely on persuasive words imbued with the kind of worldly wisdom that some among their number appeared to have prized:

For, whereas the Jews demand signs and Greeks desire wisdom, we proclaim a crucified Messiah, a stumbling block to Jews and foolishness to Gentiles, but to those who are the called, both Jews and Greeks, Christ the power of God and the wisdom of God. (1 Cor 1:22–24)

Hence, Paul explains, the approach that he was bound to take when he came to Corinth preaching the gospel:

For I decided to know nothing among you except Jesus Christ, and him crucified....My speech and my proclamation were not with plausible words of wisdom, but with a demonstration of the Spirit and of power, so that your faith might rest not on human wisdom but on the power of God. (1 Cor 2:2–5)

Paul seems to have believed that his preaching represented an enactment of Calvary for his hearers. It brought them before the power of God active in Jesus' death, which, through their response of faith, became for them the source of all the benefits of salvation:

[God] is the source of your life in Christ Jesus, who has become for us wisdom from God, and righteousness and sanctification and redemption. (1 Cor 1:30)

In this way, Paul understands the preaching of the gospel, focused on the cross, as an exercise of the creative power of God. As he writes in a long sentence rightly taken as stating the theme of Romans:

I am not ashamed of the gospel. It is the power of God leading to salvation for all who have faith, the Jew first, but also the Greek. For in it the righteousness of God stands revealed, from faith to faith. (Rom 1:16–17a)

CHRIST'S DEATH AS REVELATION OF THE FAITHFULNESS OF GOD (ROM 3:21–26)

Paul employs a range of images and motifs to describe the redemptive effects of Christ's death. We have already considered at some length passages where the primary category in this respect is that of "reconciliation" (2 Cor 5:17–19; Rom 5:6–10; also see Col 1:19–20; Eph 2:16). While, as earlier indicated, I personally believe that image to be primary, the one that has exercised most effect in subsequent Christian theology—and spirituality flowing from that theology—appears in an extended statement in Romans 3:21–26. A survey of Paul's spirituality would hardly be complete without some consideration of this—admittedly rather difficult—passage:

> But now, apart from law, the righteousness of God stands revealed, although the law and the prophets bear witness to it, the righteousness of God through faith in Jesus Christ for all who believe. For there is no distinction—for all have sinned and lack the glory of God. They are being justified as a gift by his grace through the redemption which has come about in Christ Jesus. God put him forward as a means of expiation, [operative] through faith, in [the shedding of] his blood. This was to display God's righteousness because of the passing over of sins formerly committed in the [time of] God's patience; it was [also] to display God's righteousness at the present time: that God himself is righteous and justifies the one who has faith in Jesus.

It is important to approach this passage with some awareness of how it fits into the wider context of Paul's exposition of the gospel in Romans. As we have seen, the gospel is not proclaimed on "neutral ground," so to speak; it is addressed to human beings as alienated from God and captive to the power of sin. In an extended lead-up to the passage we are considering (1:18—3:20), Paul has sought to demonstrate the universal scope of that alienation. It prevails not only in the Gentile world (1:18–32), but also, despite possession of the Law, in the Jewish world as well (Rom 2:1—3:20). Aside from and prior to the divine saving intervention in Christ, the entire world stands under the power of sin, lacking "righteousness" (see 3:9, 20, 23).

"Righteousness" (*dikaiosynē* in Greek) is a complex term in biblical usage. For our present purposes, it is sufficient to recall that it refers most basically to faithfulness in relationship, faithfulness in carrying out the requirements of the relationship. For Israel, the central relationship was, of course, the covenant with God. Set up through Moses on Mount Sinai, the key covenant requirement on Israel's side was the observance of the Law: "righteousness" through "works of the law" (Rom 3:20; Gal 2:16).

For Paul, however, coming to faith in the crucified Messiah and commitment to the gospel proceeding from such faith meant acknowledging that "all had sinned" (Rom 3:23; 5:12d), that there was no "righteousness" (covenant fidelity) on the human side at all. The Law of Moses, though "holy and just and good" (Rom 7:12) had proved incapable of preserving even Israel from sin (7:14–25; 8:3). In the face of this universal human failure in respect to covenant obligation, it might be thought that God was released from the divine side of the bargain. That, however, was not the case. Following a pattern seen over and over again in the history of Israel, failure and disloyalty on the human side did not lead God to abandon Israel. On the contrary, ever faithful to the covenant, God intervened to rescue Israel and restore the life of the people. Paul sees God's sending of the Son as the culminating instance of such saving intervention (Rom 8:3–4; Gal 4:4–5). In the face of total lack of "righteousness" (covenant fidelity) on the human side, the Christ event represents a display of divine righteousness to a supreme degree.

In the passage we are considering, Paul describes that intervention in "righteousness" language because he is presenting the gospel in Romans very much within a Jewish frame of reference where such language was applicable. He is not, as often maintained, importing imagery from the law court situation to describe the Christ event.[1] He is speaking of the divine fidelity, totally unmerited on the human side, in the language that a significant strain of the biblical tradition provided.

Paul's primary intent in Romans 3:21–26, however, is not to characterize the Christ event in a new way. His main concern is with human response. The universal lack of righteousness on the human side rules out any attempt to claim righteousness in God's sight through practice of the Law. The only appropriate response is that of faith: faith that acknowledges, on the one hand, one's complete lack of righteousness and which at the same time both discerns and surrenders to the divine gift of righteousness graciously held out to human beings in the cross of Christ.

The fact that faith in Christ rather than practice of the Law is the way to righteousness for human beings is supremely significant for Paul. It renders the divine gift of righteousness and destiny to salvation available to the Gentile world that does not possess the Law. This is the central truth that Paul, as apostle to the Gentiles, is affirming in his presentation of the gospel in Romans (1:16–17). As one "called" to be apostle to the Gentiles (Rom 1:1–5; 15:15–16),

Paul saw God's righteousness as extending beyond covenant fidelity to Israel. As Creator of the world as a whole, God was displaying in Christ righteousness to the entire human race. Hence, the gospel proclaimed by Paul, summoning the nations of the world to return through faith to right relationship with God and so to the realization of the Creator's design in their regard.

Note the repeated affirmations of the divine righteousness available in Christ to believers appearing at both the beginning (vv. 21–22) and the end (vv. 25b–26) of the passage we are considering. This affirmation is the main point Paul is seeking to communicate to his audience in the passage as a whole. In between (vv. 24–25a), he speaks more particularly of how God's action in the Christ event (his death on the cross) achieved this restoration of relationship between God and those who respond in faith. It is here that we run into language that has deeply affected Christian theology of the redemption. Interpreted in certain ways, it can promote an image of God that does not appear altogether faithful to the God revealed by Jesus. The relevant sentences read as follows:

> They are being justified as a gift by his grace through the redemption which has come about in Christ Jesus. God put him forward as a means of expiation, [operative] through faith, in [the shedding of] his blood. This was to display God's righteousness because of the passing over of sins formerly committed in the [time of] God's patience. (vv. 24–26)

The Greek word *dikaiosynē*, translated as "righteousness," is also translated as "justice" (e.g., in the *Jerusalem Bible*). Understood with the overtones of "justice" in our everyday sense, where fairness in the awarding of rewards and penalties is principally in view, the sentences in question can seem to present Christ's death as satisfying the demands of divine justice affronted by human sin. Such an understanding is reinforced when the Greek word rendered previously as "means of expiation" is taken in the sense of "propitiation," that is, as having to do with assuaging the anger of some party, whether human or divine. This leads to the view of Christ's death, especially in its painful aspect, as "satisfying" the anger of God at human sin, as changing the divine "wrath" into favor. We might recall the lines of a familiar Easter hymn:

> That guiltless Son who bought your peace
> And made his Father's anger cease.[2]

An understanding of redemption along these lines is still widely encased in the Christian imagination.

This view, however, fails to take account of several significant aspects of Paul's text. First, what is in view is a divine act of "justification" (v. 24), that is, a divine restoration of relationship between God and human beings ("they are being justified"), the gratuitous nature of which Paul doubly stresses ("as a gift by his grace"). Justification in this sense is coming about "through the redemption…in Christ Jesus." "Redemption" (*apolytrōsis*) is a word used chiefly with respect to the liberation of prisoners of war, who, as was customary in the ancient world, have been sold into slavery. It has the sense of freedom gained through the payment of a price. Here, it is natural to relate the price to the painful death of Christ on the cross, but there are no grounds for thinking of that as a price *paid* to any subject. Paul, as we have seen, thinks of the human condition as a slavery to sin. Christ liberated us from that slavery at the cost of his death on the cross. That is why his action can be described—metaphorically—as a "redemption," but the cost—his painful death—came about, not because the Father demanded "payment." It came about because of the human situation: because the divine love and reconciliation that he offered met rebuff and violence from the world.

Second, the "satisfaction" understanding does not do justice to the clearly stated initiative of God in the process: "God put him forward" (v. 24). It sets up a wedge between the work of Christ and the response of the Father, whose disposition has, it would seem, to be changed by that work. Whereas the text suggests a perfect continuity between the action of the Father and the work of the Son. Once full due is given to the divine initiative, the bizarre nature of God "satisfying" God's own wrath is apparent. The aim of the divine action is not to change an attitude in God. It is to change something on the human side: to transform human hostility and alienation into right relationship through a totally gracious (one-sided) offer of reconciliation.

Finally, Paul is likely to be using the word *hilastērion*, not in its meaning in secular Greek, where it contains a note of propitiation but in a metaphorical sense alluding to the Day of Atonement ritual in Israel. In the Greek version of the Old Testament (the Septuagint), *hilastērion* appears with reference to the golden cover placed over the ark of the covenant in the innermost recesses of the temple, the holy of holies. On the yearly Day of Atonement, the high priest sprinkled on this cover the blood of a goat slain as a sin offering on that day of forgiveness and renewal of covenant "righteousness" with God (Lev 16:15–16). It was not that the ritual "moved" God to forgive the accumulated sins of the people. The "flow" was all the other way: the ritual enacted in a tangible sacramental way God's gracious "wiping away" ("expiation") of sin, thereby restoring the covenant relationship to full vigor for the year to come. Once again, the initiative lay entirely with God, the high priest acting as God's instrument rather than representative of the people at this point.

It was probably the shedding of Christ's blood on the

cross that led to an early Christian interpretation of Christ's death in terms of the Day of Atonement in this way. Whereas the early tradition presumably related the removal of sin simply to Israel, Paul saw the matter in more universal terms. In Christ's death, God was not simply enacting, as covenant partner, a messianic Day of Atonement for Israel. As universal Creator, God was enacting a final Day of Atonement for the entire world. In this sense, the redemption effected in Christ Jesus represents an act of divine covenant fidelity ("righteousness") to all nations. The gospel proclaimed by Paul and his fellow workers makes the benefits of that divine righteousness available to all who respond in faith. Hence—to revisit the thematic statement early in Romans—his boast:

> I am not ashamed of the gospel. It is the power of God leading to salvation for all who have faith, the Jew first, but also the Greek. For in it the righteousness of God stands revealed, from faith to faith. (1:16–17a)

REFLECTION

We have considered the extended redemption statement in Romans 3:21–26 at some length because it represents one place where Paul's language can give rise to a less-than-adequate image of God, with unfortunate consequences for a spirituality associated with his name. Taken in its context, with careful attention to the divine initiative and the way key terms are being used, the passage is in full agreement with other statements of God's action in Christ that we have noted: especially the "reconciliation" formulations in 2 Corinthians 5:18–21 and later in Romans in 5:6–11. They are all ways of presenting the death of Jesus, especially in its costly aspect, as the outreach of the Creator's fidelity to an estranged world. Ultimately, what redeems the world is not the suffering of Christ but the love and obedience displayed in his willingness to take on that suffering on behalf of the entire human race. In the representative person of the New Adam, human beings can enter into a divine love so immense as to counter the entire mass of human selfishness and sin. Consequently, there is restored—or, rather, gained for the first time—the love relationship with God that was the original intent of the Creator from the start (Gen 2).

SUGGESTED SCRIPTURE

1 Corinthians 1:18—2:5; Galatians 3:1–14; 2 Corinthians 4:7–15; Hebrews 2:10–18; 4:14—5:10; 10:11–25; Isaiah 52:13—53:12; any one of the passion accounts in the Gospels

PERSONAL REFLECTION

What image of God the Father emerges for me from contemplation of Christ crucified?

Can I make my own Paul's personal avowal: "I have been crucified with Christ; and it is no longer I who live, but it is Christ who lives in me. And the life I now live in the flesh I live by faith in the Son of God, who loved me and gave himself up for me" (Gal 2:19b–20)?

Are there any ways in which the contemplation of divine love displayed in the Crucified might lead me to greater generosity in the service of God?

THE EUCHARISTIC BODY

We should be profoundly grateful that the Christian community in Corinth experienced so many problems. We would lack so much precious information and instruction from Paul had it not been necessary for him to write—at least three times that we know of (see 1 Cor 5:9)—to address issues and problems in this lively early community.

One significant aspect of early Christian life that we would lack information about, had the Corinthians celebrated it worthily, concerns the Eucharist. Both of Paul's references to the Eucharist occur in 1 Corinthians: first, a brief allusion made in the course of a warning about getting too close to idolatrous worship (10:16–17); second, a far more extensive admonition about the community's celebration of the communal meal (11:17–34). Our principal focus here will be on this second, more extended passage but, despite its brevity, the earlier reference merits consideration.

COMMUNION WITH THE LORD AND WITH THE COMMUNITY (1 COR 10:16–17)

In 1 Corinthians 8, Paul begins a lengthy response to an inquiry from the community about whether they can eat meat sold in the marketplace after having been used for sacrifice in pagan temples. This is not an issue that exercises us today, but as Paul's return to the same issue in Romans 14:1—15:6 shows, it was one that bulked large in the early Christian communities. Meat used in such sacrifices was of high quality. Its subsequent sale in the market provided a

146

valuable source of nourishment for poor people, who otherwise would not have been able to afford meat.

Paul's lengthy response across chapters 8—10 in 1 Corinthians is somewhat ambiguous. For the most part, his advice is liberal: since idols have no reality, those of mature faith, knowing this to be the case, are free to partake of such meat without injury to their commitment to Christ. If, on the other hand, their exercise of freedom in this respect might give scandal to a brother or sister whose faith was weak, causing them to fall, then a deeper exercise of freedom might lead them to curtail their freedom in this respect for the sake of the brother or sister for whom Christ died (1 Cor 8:1–13). In chapter 9, Paul digresses to provide an example of this voluntary restriction of freedom from his own policy as missionary apostle (not requiring monetary support for his own upkeep from the churches he has founded). In chapter 10, he returns to the main issue. While not going back on his original advice about eating meat sacrificed to idols (10:23–33), he does accompany it with a strong warning to keep clear of any taint of idolatrous worship (10:1–22). This is not because idols have any reality but because demons manipulate such worship for their own evil ends. It is in this context that the short eucharistic reference occurs:

> Therefore, my dear friends, flee from the worship of idols. I speak as to sensible people; judge for yourselves what I say. The cup of blessing that we bless, is it not a communion [*koinōnia*] in the blood of Christ? The bread that we break, is it not a communion [*koinōnia*] in the body of Christ? Because there is one bread, we, many though we be, are one body, for we all partake of the one bread. (10:14–17)

What is central in this short passage is the word and concept of *koinōnia*. The Greek word is variously translated in English as "sharing," "fellowship," or "communion." The last translation, "communion," has returned in the Greeting with which the celebrant begins the Eucharistic celebration in the recently revised English translation. It best catches the very deep sense of union conveyed by the Greek term *koinōnia*. *Koinōnia* refers to the union established among a number of people by their common participation in something in which they all share: the classic example would be the *koinōnia* established when, to celebrate a birthday, people share a meal or even a cake baked for this purpose.

The two short sentences that make up verses 16 and 17 show that Paul believes that the Eucharistic participation sets up *koinōnia* in two "directions": *koinōnia* in a "vertical" direction, if we can speak in such a way, with Christ, established by participation in the cup symbolizing the shedding of his blood; *koinōnia* in a "horizontal" direction with the community, established by the sharing of the "one bread." The statement in verse 17 is a comment on this latter *koinōnia*, although Paul's wider argument actually rests more on the "vertical" communion with Christ (vv. 18–22). Such communion is totally incompatible with the debased "communion" with demons that would be established by believers' sharing in idolatrous love feasts, which seems to be Paul's concern at this point.

While the stress in this short allusion to the Eucharist may be on the "vertical" union with Christ, the reference in a more "horizontal" sense to the community as constituting the "Body" (*sōma*) of Christ is significant. Paul's communities were of a mixed nature, ethnically speaking. His descriptions of the community as the Body of Christ often occur in contexts where he is sressing the overcoming of differences or the variety of gifts in the community of the new creation: 1 Corinthians 12 (see especially vv. 12–13; cf. Gal 3:26–28); Rom 12:3–8. Participation in the one bread is both an expression of the unity (*koinōnia*) between believers and a forger of that unity. One cannot participate simply as an individual, united with Christ but not with one's fellow believers. This essential unity between the vertical and horizontal dimension of the celebration features even more strongly in the second eucharistic passage, to which we now turn.

"DISCERNING THE BODY" (1 COR 11:17–34)

The early Christians celebrated the Eucharist in the context of a wider meal, which came to be known as the *Agape*. Paul's problem with the way the Corinthians were celebrating the Eucharist had in fact to do more with the circumstances of this wider meal than with the celebration of the actual sacramental rite itself. Or, to be more accurate, he felt that the way they were celebrating the former—the meal—contravened the essential meaning of the rite: as he says bitingly at the start, "It is not the Lord's Supper that you are celebrating" (v. 20). Paul recites the tradition about the Lord's institution of the Eucharist in order to remind the Corinthians of the meaning that the Lord imprinted on it, the meaning that is being frustrated by the way they are celebrating the total event and, in particular, the surrounding meal:

> Now in the following instructions I do not commend you, because when you come together it is not for the better but for the worse. For, to begin with, when you come together as a church, I hear that there are divisions among you; and to some extent I believe it….When you come together, it is not really to eat the Lord's supper. For when the time comes to eat, each of you goes ahead with your own supper, and one goes hungry and another becomes drunk. What! Do you not have homes to

eat and drink in? Or do you show contempt for the church of God and humiliate those who have nothing? What should I say to you? Should I commend you? In this matter I do not commend you! (1 Cor 11:17–22)

It is not entirely clear from Paul's description of the situation whether the abuse that he is castigating consists in the fact that the food that people bring to the celebration is not being shared or whether the problem is they are not waiting for everyone to arrive. At the end, he tells them,

> So then, my brothers and sisters, when you come together to eat, wait for one another. If you are hungry, eat at home, so that when you come together, it will not be for your condemnation. (vv. 33–34)

Not waiting for everyone to arrive is the more likely cause of Paul's complaint granted that many of the members of the community would not have been masters of their own timetable. If they were slaves or servants in lowly employment, they would not have been released from service until their masters or mistresses gave them leave. Their late arrival, then, as the celebration was well underway—and most of the food eaten—would simply reinforce consciousness of being people of inferior status. Paul suggests that the shaming of such poor and marginalized people was a greater evil than their being deprived of food—though that would not have been a light matter either. Not without a touch of scorn, perhaps, he suggests that those troubled by hunger pangs while waiting for everyone to arrive should have a snack at home beforehand (v. 22).

To address the abuse, Paul recites the Eucharistic tradition, providing us with the earliest form of it:

> For I received from the Lord what I also handed on to you, that the Lord Jesus on the night when he was betrayed took a loaf of bread, and when he had given thanks, he broke it and said, "This is my body that is for you. Do this in remembrance of me." In the same way he took the cup also, after supper, saying, "This cup is the new covenant in my blood. Do this, as often as you drink it, in remembrance of me." For as often as you eat this bread and drink the cup, you proclaim the Lord's death until he comes. (vv. 23–26)

We note the words over the bread: "This is my body that is for you" (*touto mou estin to sōma to hyper hymōn*). It is gratifying that the renewed form of eucharistic celebration following Vatican II added an echo of Paul's specification of the finality of the body: "This is my body, *which will be given up for you*," to the earlier bald statement, "This is my body." The latter placed the emphasis on the "real presence," the transformation of bread into the body of the Lord. The revised form, while not removing that meaning, added the more dynamic note that the body of Christ present in the Eucharist is the "given up for you—for the brothers and sisters—body."

There follows (v. 24c), as in Luke's version (22:19), the instruction, "Do this in memory of me." Behind this instruction lies the biblical sense of "memorial" (*zikkarōn* in Hebrew). A biblical memorial, in the form of a feast or a liturgical rite, does not merely recall some event in the past. In a genuinely sacramental way, it renders those who celebrate the feast or enact the ritual actually present to the past event. Or, to put it (perhaps more accurately) the other way around, it renders the past event present so that later generations, like their ancestors of old, may participate in it despite the passage of years. The Jewish feast of Passover, which of course is the setting for the Last Supper in the Synoptic accounts, has this

meaning. It enables Jewish people of later times to participate in the exodus, the deliverance from Egyptian foundational for Israel's identity as a people.

The words over the cup (v. 25), speak of sealing "the
new covenant in my blood." The language of "new covenant"
comes from Jeremiah 31:31, a passage mentioned earlier
when we were considering Paul's sense of movement from
slavery under the Law to freedom in the Spirit (Rom 7:14—
8:4). According to Exodus 24:7–8, Moses sealed the Sinai
covenant by sprinkling the Israelites, after they had accepted
it, with "the blood of the covenant."

> Then [Moses] took the book of the covenant, and
> read it in the hearing of the people; and they said,
> "All that the LORD has spoken we will do, and
> we will be obedient." Moses took the blood and
> dashed it on the people, and said, "See the blood of
> the covenant that the LORD has made with you in
> accordance with all these words. (24:7–8)

The form of the eucharistic tradition preserved in Mark
(14:24) and Matthew (26:27–28) actually makes mention
of "the blood of the covenant" in the words over the cup.
Luke (22:20) joins Paul in speaking of the "new covenant in
my blood." The two strands of the eucharistic tradition—the
Markan-Matthean, on the one hand, and the Pauline-Lukan,
on the other—are complementary in that they suggest that,
as the Israelites sealed their entry into the former covenant
when sprinkled with the blood of the covenant by Moses,
so believers enter a new covenant sealed by the shedding of
Jesus' blood on Calvary. With this phrase, Jesus specified at
the Last Supper the meaning of his death that would take
place the following day. It would open up to the world the
"new covenant" relationship with God promised by Jeremiah

and marked by the placing of the Spirit "within" the hearts of the people (Ezek 36:26–27; see also 2 Cor 3:6).

After this recital of the eucharistic tradition, Paul adds a comment that, again thankfully, has become one of the acclamations recited after the consecration:

> For as often as you eat this bread and drink the cup,
> you proclaim the Lord's death until he comes. (v. 26)

The final phrase, "until he comes," specifies the time-reference of the eucharistic rite that Jesus is inaugurating: it is for the "in-between" time in which believers live, that is, the space of time from his "departure" in death, resurrection, and ascension, until his return at the end of time. The Eucharist, as "memorial" in the biblical sense, will be the way in which believers participate in the saving effects of his death during this period.

One wonders how many believers today, when reciting the acclamation based on Paul's final comment about "proclaiming the Lord's death until he comes," really appreciate the full meaning of what they are saying. It is not just a matter of remembering the death of Jesus in a general kind of way. It is a matter of appreciating, as the words over the bread in particular indicate, that his death was a death "for us"—a death that Jesus died because he "loved us and gave himself up for us" (see Gal 2:20). We proclaim, then, not only the death of Jesus as a historical fact. More than that, we proclaim the divine love that he displayed in his death—in all the ways that so many Pauline passages reveal.

Now, let us see how Paul applies this recall of the institution narrative to the conduct of the Corinthians in their celebration:

> Whoever, therefore, eats the bread or drinks the
> cup of the Lord in an unworthy manner will be

> answerable for the body and blood of the Lord.
> Examine yourselves, and only then eat of the bread
> and drink of the cup. For all who eat and drink
> without discerning the body, eat and drink judg-
> ment against themselves. (vv. 27–29)

The phrase in this warning that has attracted most comment
is the participial phrase in the last verse, "without discerning
the body" (*mē diakrinōn to sōma*). The Catholic tradition,
with its strongly realistic sense of the presence of the Lord
in the Eucharist, has seen here an indication precisely of that
real presence: Paul is warning the Corinthians against failing
to distinguish the now-consecrated bread from ordinary bread.
There is nothing against this interpretation and it should
certainly be retained. However, it should not exclude another
interpretation that has, historically, been more congenial to the
Protestant tradition, namely, a "social" interpretation where
the "body" to be discerned is the "body of the Lord" in the
shape of the community making up the Body of Christ (see
1 Cor 12:12–13). The Corinthians are failing to grasp that,
when they meet together to celebrate the *Agape* meal and
the eucharistic rite within it, they are not simply a collection
of individuals; they meet as the "body of the Lord." Their
failure to wait for each one to gather, their getting ahead with
the food they have personally brought rather than sharing it,
their depriving and shaming the poor: in all these ways, their
behavior implies a failure to "discern the body of the Lord" in
this "social" sense. They are not really celebrating the Supper
in the meaning imprinted on it by the Lord, whose death in
love poured out for all it celebrates, proclaims, and enacts.

These two understandings of "discerning the body"—
the "real presence" and the "social"—are, in fact, complementary. The Lord is truly present in the consecrated bread, but

he is present in the dynamic sense of the one who gave his life in love. To eat with discernment is to allow oneself to be caught up in the rhythm of that divine love.

REFLECTION

There is a strong foundation for a specifically priestly spirituality here. As celebrants of the Eucharist, acting at the moment of consecration *in persona Christi*, priests proclaim, "This is my body, given for you." The proclamation surely imposes an obligation to live life in the body in conformity with the dynamic rhythm of Christ's self-sacrificial love. There is no reason, however, for not extending the same sense of being drawn into the rhythm of that love to all recipients of the body and blood of the Lord—both on the individual level but also on the level of the eucharistic community as a whole.

Although Paul does not return to the motif of *koinōnia* when he admonishes the Corinthians for the way they are celebrating the Eucharist, it is probably not far below the surface. Here, as so often, we see his thought coming back to the love displayed in Christ's death, which is, of course, for him simply the "extension" of the divine love for the world that lies behind his entire mission. All in all, the two eucharistic texts in 1 Corinthians—despite the brevity of the one in chapter 10—place a Pauline spirituality on a firmly eucharistic base.

SUGGESTED SCRIPTURE

1 Corinthians 8:1–13; 10:14–17; 11:17–34; Romans 12:1–13; 13:8–14; 14:7–13; 15:1–6; Luke 22:14–20, 24–27; John 6:51–58

PERSONAL REFLECTION

Is there anything in my life that could correspond to a "worship of idols," incompatible with the *koinōnia* with Christ established in the Eucharist?

What does "discerning the body" mean for me in receiving the Eucharist?

What does it mean for the community/church in which I worship?

How can I live more "eucharistically"?

DAY 8

RESURRECTION AND MISSION

It is natural to think of the appearances of the risen Lord as Jesus "coming back" from the dead into the world as we know it. The earliest believers, however, hardly understood the resurrection in that way. For them, and particularly for Paul, it was not so much Jesus coming back into the present world as a glimpse of a new world coming to be as a result of his death and resurrection. The "sight" of the risen Lord was, in fact, a window into the new creation—more specifically, a vision of a new possibility for humanity in the person of the "Last Adam," now become "life-giving Spirit" (1 Cor 15:45).

In light of this understanding, let us consider more intentionally Paul's understanding of the resurrection of Jesus and its consequences for understanding the mission and ministry of the church. This means examining the first half of 1 Corinthians 15 in somewhat greater detail than we have hitherto.

PAUL'S WITNESS TO THE RESURRECTION (1 COR 15:12–19)

First, however, let us consider what provoked Paul to treat of the resurrection in this splendid chapter at such length. As in regard to the eucharistic tradition (1 Cor 11:17–34), we should be profoundly grateful that the Corinthian church had problems in so many areas of its life. Otherwise, we would not have these responses of Paul, so rich in theology and information about the early years of the church. Here, the indication of what he is responding to comes in verse 12:

> Now if Christ is proclaimed as raised from the dead, how can some of you say there is no resurrection of the dead?

Some of the community are saying that there is no resurrection of the dead. There seems to have been a widespread belief in the very earliest days of the Christian communities that the baptized would not suffer death but would remain alive until the return of Christ in glory on the last day. They believed that their baptismal death with Christ removed the destiny to death that hung over them as a penalty for sin (the legacy of Adam, ratified by their own personal sinning [Rom 5:12]). Hence, they concluded that they would not die but stay around until taken up by the Lord after his return in glory to the earth. When members of the community did in fact begin to die, this created a problem: had they simply dropped out of salvation? Understandably, such a conclusion would cause great grief to their relatives and others who mourned them. Paul first addressed this issue in the fourth chapter of his earliest letter, 1 Thessalonians (4:13–18). There he does so in terms of a rather literalistic eschatology—the Lord descending from heaven at the sound of God's trumpet and the faithful being caught up to meet him "in the air" (vv. 16–17).

Paul addresses the same problem in 1 Corinthians, but his understanding of the events of the end of time has moved on. He now formulates a more sophisticated understanding of how both the living and dead can share in the risen existence of the Lord.[1] His argument hinges on the absolute unity between the resurrection of Christ and that of the faithful departed. If you deny one, you deny the other. This argument actually reflects the Jewish understanding of resurrection at the time of Jesus and Paul. Not all Jews, of course, believed in the resurrection of the dead. The party of the Sadduccees notoriously did not, and we find Jesus in controversy with them on this score in the Synoptic Gospels (Matt 22:23–33; Mark 12:18–27; Luke 20:27–40). It was, however, a central tenet of the Pharisees party, to which, of course, Paul belonged in his pre-Christian career. Jewish belief in resurrection, however, which was first clearly signaled in the Book of Daniel (12:1–2), was belief in a resurrection of the righteous to take place simultaneously at the end of time. This was, then, a point where early Christian belief had to part company with the conventional Jewish understanding. Christians believed that, though Christ had already been raised, the resurrection of the rest of the faithful remained a matter of hope. Nonetheless, despite the time gap, the two instances of resurrection—that of Christ and that of the faithful departed—were inescapably bound together, the one with the other.

This connection is pivotal to Paul's case. He first reminds the Corinthians of their belief in the resurrection of Christ, which is the bedrock of their faith. He does so by recalling what would appear to be the little creed to which they first gave belief (vv. 3–5), "updating" it by adding to the list of resurrection witnesses (vv. 5–7), concluding with his own meeting with the risen Lord (vv. 8–10), and an assertion of the common faith (v. 11). Then, in a kind of *argumentum ad hominem*, he points out the total incompatibility between this belief in the resurrection of Christ and the denial of the resurrection of the dead. They are so bound up with one another that to deny the resurrection of the faithful is to deny the resurrection of Christ.

If there is no resurrection of the dead, then Christ has not been raised; and if Christ has not been raised, then our proclamation has been in vain and your faith has been in vain. We are even found to be misrepresenting God, because we testified of God that he raised Christ—whom he did not raise if it is true that the dead are not raised. For if the dead are not raised, then Christ has not been raised. If Christ has not been raised, your faith is futile and you are still in your sins. Then those also who have died in Christ have perished. If for this life only we have hoped in Christ, we are of all people most to be pitied. (vv. 13–19)

Note how Paul works back from denial of the resurrection of Christ through all the fatal consequences that follow, right back to "you are still in your sins" (v. 17). God's raising of Christ is not simply something for Christ himself. As Paul says in Romans 4:25, "Christ died for our sins and was raised for our justification," that is, for our acquittal from sin and our being set on the path to eternal life. Denial of the resurrection of the dead puts all this in jeopardy.

THE MESSIANIC REIGN OF THE RISEN LORD (1 COR 15:20–28)

To place belief in the resurrection on a secure footing, Paul has to address the issue of the "time gap" between the resurrection of Christ and that of the faithful—a time gap not anticipated, as we have seen, in conventional Jewish belief. He does so in 1 Corinthians 15:20–28. (Later, in vv. 35–53, he will address the "how" of resurrection, that is, the nature of risen *bodily* existence, which need not concern us here.)

But in fact Christ has been raised from the dead,
the first fruits of those who have died. For since
death came through a human being, the resurrection of the dead has also come through a human
being; for as all die in Adam, so all will be made
alive in Christ. But each in his own order: Christ
the first fruits, then at his coming those who
belong to Christ. Then comes the end, when he
hands over the kingdom to God the Father, after he
has destroyed every ruler and every authority and
power. For he must rule until he has put all his enemies under his feet. The last enemy to be destroyed
is death. For "*God has put all things in subjection
under his feet.*" But when it says, "*All things are put
in subjection,*" it is plain that this does not include
the one who put all things in subjection under him.
When all things are subjected to him, then the Son
himself will also be subjected to the one who put
all things in subjection under him, so that God may
be all in all. (1 Cor 15:20–28)

Paul begins (v. 20b) by speaking of the risen Christ as "the
first fruits [*aparchē*] of those who have died." The image of
"first fruits" (see Rom 8:23; 11:16; 16:5; 1 Cor 16:15; also see
2 Thess 2:13) comes from the harvest ritual of Israel. Each
Israelite was obliged to set aside a specified portion of the
harvest as a gesture of thanksgiving to God (Num 15:18–21).
The portion implied thanksgiving for the entire harvest and
acknowledgment that it was all God's gift. In fact, Paul sees
God acting in accordance with this ritual: God has raised
Jesus from the dead as "first fruits" of the full "harvest" that is
to follow. His resurrection is in effect a divine pledge to raise
those "in Christ" as well.

In verses 21–22, the "Adam" Christology comes to the
surface again. If "in Adam," that is, as a legacy from Adam, all

have a destiny to death, so "all will be made alive in Christ." "All" here in the latter case does not necessarily mean all human beings without exception. "All" stands over against the individual figure, Adam or Christ, each of whom has universal significance—for good or ill—for others (see Rom 5:12–21).

Paul then addresses (vv. 23–28) the issue of the time gap between the resurrection of Christ and that of believers. These eschatological events will occur in a certain "order" or "rank" (*tagma*).[2] First comes Christ, the "first fruits," as previously explained; only after an interval ("then" [*eita*]) will come "those who belong to Christ." This will occur at "the end," that is, the eschaton, when Christ returns in glory to hand over the kingdom to God the Father, after destroying everything opposed to God ("every ruler, authority and power"). To drive home the point about the interval, Paul focuses for a moment on what Christ is doing during that interval before he hands over the kingdom to the Father. While the logic is clear, the explanation doesn't follow the actual time sequence. Paul mentions what will happen at "the end" (v. 24) before explaining what Christ will be doing before that moment (vv. 25–27). What Christ will be doing is "ruling," that is, actively exercising his messianic power to overcome every power opposed to God, so that, his messianic task completed, he can hand over "the kingdom," that is, the world reclaimed for God, to the Father who sent him on this mission (v. 28).

What we need to be aware of here is how the early believers had to reconfigure the prevailing understanding of the Messiah's reign in conventional Jewish expectation. The latter awaited a righteous ruler of David's line—not in any sense a divine figure—who would liberate the people from foreign rule (notably, that of Rome) and set up a renewed Israel in righteousness, prosperity, and peace. The evidence of the Gospels shows that, throughout his public mission, Jesus struggled to disassociate himself from such expectations (see Mark 8:27–33 and parallels; Acts 1:6–7). For him, the "kingdom" or "rule of God" was more about renewed relationship with God than about expelling the Romans. Nonetheless, after his death—under a sign that, mockingly, proclaimed him "King of the Jews"—and in light of belief that God had raised him from the dead, Jesus' disciples did come to confess him as "Messiah" ("Christ").

Applied to Jesus, the confession required understanding messiahship in a radically new way. Transferred from earth to heaven, his "installation" as messianic king took place—postresurrection—in his exaltation and ascension to God's right hand, with the opening verse of the messianic psalm, Psalm 110 (109), providing scriptural validation:

> The LORD says to my lord,
> "Sit at my right hand
> until I make your enemies your footstool." (v. 1)[3]

This heavenly installation, however, did not mean removal from influence on earth. On the contrary, as "life-giving Spirit" (1 Cor 15:45), the risen Lord continues to exercise his redemptive messianic mission on earth, reclaiming the world for the rule ("kingdom") of God from all the forces alien to God that presently run in human affairs (v. 24c). The "last enemy" to be destroyed is death (v. 26).[4] It is only when death itself has been destroyed that the moment of general resurrection will arrive. Hence, the time gap that has to prevail between the resurrection of the Lord and that of the faithful.

In connection with this "destruction" of death, Paul adds a comment rich in theological implications. In verse 27, he quotes Psalm 8, a psalm that uniquely describes the dignity and role of human beings in the world. It provides, in fact, a poetic development of the description in Genesis 1:26–28 of the creation of human beings. Here is a relevant part of the psalm:

> When I see the heavens, the work of your hands,
> the moon and the stars which you arranged;
> what is man that you should keep him in mind,
> mortal man that you care for him?
> Yet you have made him little less than a god,
> with glory and honor you crowned him,
> gave him power over the works of your hand,
> put all things under his feet. (Ps 8:4–7)[5]

Note the final phrase, "put all things under his feet." In 1 Corinthians 15:27, Paul quotes this phrase from Psalm 8:7 with reference to the messianic rule of Christ (see also Phil 3:21). He associates it with "make your enemies your footstool" in Psalm 110:1, likewise understood messianically. If "your enemies" (here the powers hostile to God) are made your "footstool," then they are "under your feet." The allusion in 1 Corinthians 15:27 to this motif emanating from the two psalms presents the messianic reign of the risen Lord as fulfilling the role sketched out for human beings in the universe according to Psalm 8 (also see Gen 1:26–28). The "Adam" Christology is still present: the risen Lord, as true image (*eikōn*) of God (2 Cor 3:18; 4:4; Col 1:15; 3:10), is the founder and model of a renewed humanity in which the original design of the Creator for human beings and the universe (Gen 1:26–28; Ps 8) is coming true. This is the "new creation" or rather, the original creation being rescued from chaos and destruction and brought to realization for the first time. We see this in connection with 2 Corinthians 5:17:

> So if anyone is in Christ, there is a new creation: everything old has passed away; see, everything has become new!

To be baptized "into Christ" is to leave the lineage of the old Adam and enter that of the New, whose messianic reign creates a new possibility for human beings and the world.

THE GIFTS OF THE SPIRIT AT THE SERVICE OF THE NEW CREATION (1 COR 12—14)

A great Lutheran interpreter of Paul of the last century, Ernst Käsemann, had a particular understanding of the gifts of the Spirit (the *charismata*) within this understanding of the messianic reign of Christ. Käsemann interpreted Paul's discussion of the gifts of the Spirit in 1 Corinthians 12—14 as implying that the distinctive gift of the Spirit given to each and every believer represented a particular instantiation of Christ's exercise, through the Spirit, of his ongoing messianic mission in the church and in the world.[6] Paul, of course, in these chapters of the letter is not giving systematic instruction so much as insisting that there is a variety of gifts of the Spirit. He is tackling and seeking to correct the Corinthians' preference for the more spectacular gifts, notably the gift of tongues. In fact, Paul ranks the gifts in a way that puts tongues rather low down on the scale (12:7–10). The ruling criterion of value is what builds up the community rather than what enhances the individual's self-image:

> Now there are varieties of gifts, but the same *Spirit*;
> and there are varieties of services, but the same *Lord*;
> and there are varieties of activities, but it is the same
>   *God* who activates all of them in everyone.
> To each is given the manifestation of the Spirit for the
>   common good. (1 Cor 12:4–7)

Once again, we note here how Paul's argument falls into a trinitarian shape: "same Spirit," "same Lord," "same God" (the

Father). The "building up" of the community through the gifts is ultimately the work of the Trinity (see Rom 8:3–4). In Pauline theology, the triune God does not dwell in remote mystery. The Trinity is here among us building up the community through the work of the Spirit.

In this connection, Paul appeals (vv. 12–14) to the familiar image of a group of people as making up a "body":

> For just as the body is one and has many members, and all the members of the body, though many, are one body, so it is with the Christ. For in the one Spirit we were all baptized into one body—Jews or Greeks, slaves or free—and we were all made to drink of one Spirit. (1 Cor 12:12–13)

The final phrase of verse 12, "so it is with the Christ," makes clear that "body" (*sōma*) here does not function simply as an image but expresses the reality of believers incorporated into the person of the risen Lord. There is an echo of the communion (*koinōnia*) established and enacted in the eucharistic celebration (1 Cor 10:16–17; 11:29). Similarly, there is a reminder of the suppression in Christ of the differences (ethnic and social) that belong to the old, passing era (see Gal 3:27–28). Such differences should no longer determine attitudes and behavior in the new creation.

Without going into the various gifts, we should note, in a way that may bring some comfort to those engaged in ministry involving administration, that such a responsibility (*kybernēsis* [literally, "governance"]) does find a place within Paul's list, and that it actually precedes the gift of tongues (v. 28)! Administration—or perhaps we should say the capacity to perform this ministry in a way that builds up the community—is a gift of the Spirit.

As noted earlier, Käsemann's view is that the gifts distributed by the Spirit are extensions or outworkings of the risen Lord's messianic rule. The actual word used for "gift" of the Spirit is *charisma*, that is, a particular instance of the *charis*, the grace of God, the "force," if that is the appropriate word, behind the whole redemptive act of God to bring the world to the new creation. Although Paul in 1 Corinthians 12 and 14 relates such gifts to the building up of the believing community, there is no good reason not to see them extending to the wider world as well: in other words, to see them as part of the "subjection" of all things, especially forces hostile to the divine design to humanize the world preparatory to Christ's handing over the kingdom to the Father (1 Cor 15:24).[7]

REFLECTION

All this is what encounter with the risen Lord and "being captured" for a share in his messianic mission meant for Paul. Related to the vocation of believers today, it may appear utopian in the extreme—especially in the present state of the world. Although expressed in very different language, it is not all that far removed from the great Ignatian meditations of the Call of the King and the Two Standards. Those meditations summon us to discern how best we may allow ourselves to be instruments of the messianic reign of Christ through the gift of the Spirit given to each one.

SUGGESTED SCRIPTURE

1 Corinthians 12:1–30; 14:1–25; 15:12–28; Ephesians 1:20–23; 4:4–13; 1 Thessalonians 1:2–10; 5:1–11; Mark 10:17–22

PERSONAL REFLECTION

How does Paul's sense of the ongoing messianic "rule" of the
risen Christ affect my view of the world?

How can I discern the particular gift (*charisma*) of the Spirit
that has been given to me within this sense of Christ's
reclaiming the world for God?

How might I live out this gift more effectively in union with
the risen Lord?

How does my ministry help others to discern and exercise
effectively their own gifts of the Spirit within the
community?

THE VICTORY OF GOD'S LOVE

As is well known, St. Ignatius concludes the program of the *Spiritual Exercises* with a prayer exercise titled "Contemplation for Obtaining Love" (§§230–37). The second "prelude" to this exercise indicates the grace to be sought: "an interior knowledge of the many and great benefits I have received, that, thoroughly grateful, I may in all things love and serve the divine majesty" (§233). This petition makes clear that the love to be obtained as the aim of the exercise is an increased love for God on the part of the retreatant as a consequence of becoming more profoundly grateful for all that he or she has received from God.[8]

The sense of love proceeding from gratitude has much in common with a statement Paul makes in passing to the Corinthians about the goal of his entire ministry:

> Yes, everything is for your sake, so that grace, as it extends to more and more people, may increase thanksgiving, to the glory of God. (2 Cor 4:15)

Grace increases thanksgiving, which, presumably—although Paul does not explicitly say so—leads to love.[9]

In connection with the theme of love, the Pauline passage that comes most readily to mind is the famous praise (*encomium*) of love that makes up the whole of 1 Corinthians 13. It is certainly the most popular Pauline text for weddings. The love expressed in the passage is human love: human love for God that displays itself in an active, unfeigned love for the neighbor. Toward the climax of the passage (vv. 8–13), love is praised beyond all other gifts and virtues, even beyond its fellows, "faith" and "hope," in the famous triad (v. 13). Love is "greater" than these because, while faith and hope "remain" in the present ("in-between") time, they will not apply in the fullness of salvation when partial vision ("as in a mirror") will have given way to the sight of God face to face (v. 12). Love, however, will continue in an endless exchange of love with God.

The focus on human love in 1 Corinthians 13 provides a useful checklist of love in action: described by Paul in both negative contrast and positive affirmation (vv. 1–7).[10] The passage, then, well illustrates the Ignatian dictum at the head of the *Contemplatio* that love ought to be found in deeds rather than in words (§230). Leaving the passage for practical personal reflection, let us now focus more intentionally on Paul's sense of God's love for us. When grasped with the "interior knowledge" of which Ignatius speaks, the hope is that this will draw us ever more deeply into the eternal exchange that renders love the greatest of all the gifts.

CAUGHT UP IN GOD'S UNFOLDING PLAN (ROM 8:28–30)

We have seen how consideration of God's love provided what might be called the "engine" of Paul's argument for hope that is the pervasive theme of Romans 5—8. Paul stirs up this consideration explicitly at the beginning (Rom 5:1–11): "Hope will not let us down because the love of God has been poured out into our hearts through the Holy Spirit that has been given to us" (v. 5). He returns to the same theme very notably in the conclusion (Rom 8:31–39). Before considering that well-loved passage, it will be helpful to consider the immediately preceding sentences (8:28–30). Here, too, there is much richness for our purpose.

The statement that opens this small passage, "We know that all things work together for the [ultimate] good of those who love God, those called according to his purpose" (v. 28), is often quoted. It actually reproduces an axiom of the Jewish tradition expressing the sense that, under God's providence for the elect ("those who love God"), "all things" conspire together to bring about "good." "All things" could include the nonhuman remainder of creation, the "groaning" of which Paul has just adduced as a witness to hope (vv. 19–22). More likely, however, the reference is to the sufferings of the present time that form the context for hope. All things being equal, these sufferings would be considered not "good," but "evil." But for those whose lives are enveloped by God's love, even negative things can work for "good," that is, the full realization of God's purpose in their regard.

Here, and in the sentence to follow, we touch on Paul's understanding that behind every human life lies a divine purpose or plan. The doctrine of predestination has been an unhappy legacy that some strains of Christianity have derived from Paul—to some extent from this passage in Romans 8, but more particularly from a later section in chapter 9 (vv. 10–29). Its origins lie in Israel's sense of being the chosen people of God, set apart from other nations. The more inclusive strains of the biblical tradition (e.g., Isa 42:6; 49:6) saw this privilege as giving Israel a responsibility and role before other nations: to model before them belief in one God and living human life as the Creator intended it to be led (see Jer 29:4–7). Christianity inherited this sense of election from Judaism. One of Paul's most difficult tasks was explaining how, as an effect of the saving mission of the Son, believers from the nations of the world were now to be included in God's chosen people without displacing the special position of Israel.[11] As in the case of his own vocation and call, Paul saw this choice as one taken in the eternity of God.

The important thing is to understand this sense of predestination positively and not negatively. It is a choice ultimately for all, rather than a choice for some and not for others—just as God's choice of Israel was ultimately a choice, as Creator, for the nations of the world, not an exclusion of them. When the chips are down, election—and the unfolding divine plan for individuals and the world that it connotes—simply expresses the reality of a divine love that precedes both the creation of the world and the coming into being of every human life.

Of course, as we considered earlier in our discussion of Creation, divine love has to cope with human freedom. Has God a definite, determined plan for every human life? Some language about "vocations" to the priesthood and religious life, as well as some explanations of finding God's will for one's life in the *Spiritual Exercises*, can suggest that to be the case. Personally, I've grown uneasy with such an understanding. One sympathizes with Tevye, the humble milkman in the musical *Fiddler on the Roof*, who asks God whether it would ruin some vast, eternal plan if he were a wealthy man! Has God got some "vast eternal plan" for each of us that he is dangling before us in the hope that we will catch up with it and live accordingly? I believe God acts more like good parents who wish the very best for their children as they grow to adulthood but who do not try to determine their life choices for them—that they should study medicine or be a professional golfer, and so on. Rather, wise parents would hope that, growing to mature adult freedom, their children would make choices that implement good values and lead to the happiness that only richness in relationship can bestow. Love is a force, an attraction, but love is the only "force" that sets the loved one free, rather than constraining or imprisoning. The *Spiritual Exercises* are centrally focused on making a choice—in technical language, an "election" (§§1, 21, 69). The aim is that the choice be made in maximal freedom—freedom, as Ignatius would have it, from "inordinate attachments"—and, above all, in the context of a deep relationship with God, an awareness of the tug of divine grace, and readiness to give oneself to the divine project to rescue the world from violence and sin in the person of Christ.

It is the inexorable unfolding of this divine project that Paul sets out in verses 29–30, employing the "step-like" rhetoric that we have seen earlier (5:3–4):

> Because those whom he *chose beforehand*,
>> he also *preordained*
>>> that they should become sharers in the image of his Son,
>>> that he might become the firstborn among many brothers [and sisters].
> And those whom he *preordained*,
>> these he also *called*,
>> and those whom he *called*,
>>> these he also *justified*,
>> and those whom he *justified*,
>>> these he has also *glorified*.

"Chose beforehand" is an attempt to render the more literal *foreknew*, which sounds odd in English. Behind the expression lies the biblical (Hebrew) sense of "knowledge" as "choice," so *foreknew* conveys the sense of election. The translation "preordained" attempts to avoid the term *predestined* with its negative historical baggage, and express God's saving will in the positive and open sense just explained.

Only in the case of this verb, "preordained," does Paul break into the step-like sequence of verbs in the past tense to spell out the intended destiny: "…that they should become sharers in the image (*eikōn*) of his Son" (v. 29b). We are back here with the sense of the risen Christ as the true *eikōn* or image of God (2 Cor 4:4; Col 1:15). The expression translated "sharers" (*symmorphous*) is a strong one. It does not mean simply becoming like Christ in general. Beyond mere likeness, it suggests participation in the image of God that the Son *is*. As Son of God and "last Adam" (1 Cor 15:45), the risen Lord displays and recaptures for humanity the dignity of being created in the divine image according to the original design of the Creator that has been frustrated by sin. We recall the long, theologically freighted sentence in 2 Corinthians 3:18 describing the process of our being conformed to that image through the action of the Spirit:

> And all of us, with unveiled faces, seeing the glory of the Lord as though reflected in a mirror, are being transformed into the same image from one degree of glory to another; for this comes from the Lord, the Spirit. (v. 18)

When other human beings attain the same risen state, then Christ will no longer be the sole offspring of God; rather, he will be "firstborn" within a large family (Rom 8:29c), surrounded, in his risen glory, by a large company of "brothers and sisters" who share his filial status in relation to God.

This, then, is God's predestination in our regard: that we be conformed to the risen glory of Christ. Paul does not mean to be any more determined or definite about the future of each of us than that. Admirably, while being very certain about the hope that rests on God's love, Paul remains content to be agnostic about the details of the future God has in store for us. We do not find in him any of the speculation about heavenly existence that one sees in Jewish apocalyptic texts of the time and also in certain strands of later Christian theology.[12]

The remaining verbs of the "step-like" sequence (v. 30) simply assert the extent to which the realization of the divine plan is already underway and in fact achieved. "Calling" refers to the proclamation of the gospel that Paul is furthering throughout the world. Those who have responded in faith to that calling have been "justified" in the sense of being already "right with God." The tense of the final verb, "glorified," is at first sight odd or at least daring. Surely, we are still on the way to "glory"; earlier (5:2), Paul had spoken of glory as a matter of hope. Here, he places the end of the process in the past tense as an assertion of certainty: the unfolding of the divine design to reclaim the human race for its original "Adamic" dignity is so inexorable and already so advanced that it is reasonable to speak of its completion—"glory"—as already attained.[13]

The resurrection of Christ is not, then, an *exception* or an *irruption* into the normal course of human affairs. It is the paradigm and pledge of a divine love leading humanity to reach its proper goal when the "sin" story told in Adam is overtaken and consumed by the "grace" story told in Christ. And not only humanity: the wider context (Rom 8:18–22, in particular), suggests the inclusion of the nonhuman created world within the scope of that divine design—as in the original account of Creation (Gen 1:26–28).

THE COMING VICTORY OF GOD'S LOVE (8:31–39)

The concluding passage (Rom 8:31–39) may rival the hymn to love in 1 Corinthians 13 as the all-time favorite text of Paul. At his rhetorical best, the Apostle rounds off his argument for hope with a defiant challenge to any power or circumstance that might seem to separate believers from God's triumphant love:

What then shall we say to this? If God is for us, who can be against us? He who did not spare his own Son but handed him over for us all, how will he not also give us everything else along with him? Who will bring a charge against God's chosen ones? It is God who acquits us. Who will condemn? It is Christ

[Jesus] who died, rather, was raised, who also is at the right hand of God, who indeed intercedes for us. What will separate us from the love of Christ? Will anguish, or distress, or persecution, or famine, or nakedness, or peril, or the sword? *As it is written: "For your sake we are being slain all the day; we are looked upon as sheep to be slaughtered."* No, in all these things we conquer overwhelmingly through him who loved us. For I am convinced that neither death, nor life, nor angels, nor principalities, nor present things, nor future things, nor powers, nor height, nor depth, nor any other creature will be able to separate us from the love of God that comes to us in Christ Jesus our Lord. (Rom 8:31–39)

We recall that chapter 8 began with the bold assertion that "there is now no condemnation for those who are in Christ Jesus" (v. 1). Within the apocalyptic framework that is ever the background of Paul's thought, the "condemnation" ruled out here would be a verdict that would be given at the coming great judgment. In the present passage, Paul imaginatively evokes that great assize, puts believers on trial, so to speak, and dares any power to challenge the verdict of acquittal (justification) already given by God. Above all, the continuing reality of suffering in present Christian life cannot be interpreted as a sign of divine disfavor and an indication that believers are in for a rough time at the judgment. Nothing and no one can separate believers from the love of God already so powerfully displayed in Christ.

The opening phrase, "If God is for us…" (v. 31b), could almost stand as the theme of the entire letter. Echoing earlier statements about God's "righteousness" (1:17; 3:21–26; see also 2 Cor 5:21), Paul thinks of God the Creator as eternally faithful, eternally "on the side of" human beings, even when they are unfaithful, indeed "hostile" to God (Rom 5:10).

Returning to the logic of the passage with which the entire section of the letter began (5:1–11), Paul evokes the extraordinary cost of what God has already done in order to assert absolute confidence that God will see the process through to completion. The phrase "[God] did not spare his own Son" (v. 32) evokes the Greek translation (LXX) of Genesis 22:16, where the angel who stays Abraham's hand from slaying his son Isaac praises him for being prepared "not to spare" his own beloved son. Paul's suggestion seems to be that, what God did not in the end require of Abraham, God did require of himself: the "giving up" to death of his own Son, Jesus. Nowhere else does Paul express the divine vulnerability displayed in the Christ event so poignantly. The extremity of divine love already shown in that event, when in fact we were "sinners" and "hostile" (5:6–10), guarantees that God will be "for us" to the end, will give us "all things" with him, namely, the full residue of salvation. Evoking more explicitly the final court scene (vv. 33–34), Paul defies any being to get up and bring a charge against the elect, when God has already delivered a verdict of acquittal, and when the defense attorney is no other than the risen Lord himself.

The perspective then moves from the heavenly court to the suffering situation that is the lot of believers' lives in the present (vv. 35–39). As earlier (5:1–11), the abiding issue is how that suffering is to be interpreted. Are the trials listed at length in verse 35 to be regarded as punishments that God allows angelic powers to inflict on believers? Are they signs, therefore, of a distance, indeed a separation, from divine love? Or is it, in fact, the exact opposite? The key phrase comes at the beginning of the quotation of Psalm 44:22 (LXX 43:23) in verse 36: "*For your sake*, we are being slain all the day." The sufferings listed come about not because believers are separated from God but precisely because of their union with

Christ, whose suffering they are sharing in order, in due course, to share his glorification (v. 17).

The closing sentences (vv. 37–39) evoke the scene of a victorious general's triumphant procession through Rome. In all these trials, we conquer overwhelmingly (literally, "we are hyper-conquerors") through the One (Christ) who has loved us (see Gal 2:20). Neither the trials themselves ("death, life"), nor the powers that may be thought to stand behind them ("angels, principalities," and so on), whether in present or future, can come between us and the love of God made manifest in Christ Jesus, our Lord. The list reflects the worldview of Paul's day, where various spiritual or demonic powers were seen as manipulating social and political forces prevailing in the present world, including above all, the empire of Rome. While the victory is not yet complete, these are the forces that will be compelled in the end to walk captive in the triumphant procession of Christ (see Col 2:15; Eph 1:20–23).

REFLECTION

We may not share the worldview behind Paul's list, but we can surely add items that we see as threatening us here and now. In this way, we can bring our own lives under the scope of his overwhelming confidence that all trials that believers endure are totally encompassed within the faithful love of God and built into the eventual realization of the divine saving purpose in our regard. Enveloped within that divine purpose and grasped by a liberating sense of God's love, we may make Ignatius's prayer our own:

Take, Lord, and receive all my liberty, my memory, my understanding, my entire will. Whatever I have and possess is your gift to me. To you, Lord, I restore all, to be disposed according to your will.

Give me only your love and your grace; with these I am rich enough and desire nothing more. (*Spiritual Exercises*, §234)[14]

SUGGESTED SCRIPTURE

1 Corinthians 3:21–23; 13:1–13; Romans 8:28–30; 8:31–39; 2 Corinthians 4:7–18; Ephesians 1:3–14; Luke 1:46–55 (Magnificat)

PERSONAL REFLECTION

Would I add or subtract any items from Paul's list of the qualities of "love" in 1 Corinthians 13?

How have "all things," including painful things, "worked together unto good" (Rom 8:28) in my life?

How is my life enveloped in a saving plan of God?

What things or experiences might I add to Paul's list of things that "will not separate us from God's love" (Rom 8:35, 38–39)?

How can I make the "Take, Lord, and receive" prayer of St. Ignatius my own?

NOTES

INTRODUCTION

1.   See Rom 1:8–12; 1 Cor 1:4–9; 2 Cor 1:3–7; Phil 1:3–11; Col 3:3–14; 1 Thess 1:2–10; Phlm 4–7. The exception is the Letter to the Galatians: Paul is so angry about the community's falling away from the gospel that he feels he has nothing to thank God for in their regard (see Gal 1:6–9; 3:1).

2.   See Ruth Burrows, *Guidelines for Mystical Prayer* (London: Burns & Oates, 1976; reprinted 2007), 83.

"WHAT ARE YOU DOING HERE, ELIJAH?" (1 KGS 19:1–16)

1.   In the scene recorded in the Gospels when the disciples are in the boat rowing against a headwind and Jesus comes to them walking on the water, we are told he made as if "to pass by," indicating not an intention literally to move on beyond them but to offer a sense of divine presence: "It is I; fear not" (Matt 14:27; Mark 6:50; John 6:20).

2.   The Hebrew reads *qol demamah raqqah*. The first word clearly has the sense of "sound" or "voice"; the second can mean "calm"/"stillness" (as in Ps 107:29) as well as "silence" (as in Job 4:16); the third word, an adjective, has the range "thin," "fine," "soft." The *Jerusalem Bible* translation, "sound of a gentle breeze," follows the Greek translation (LXX), but the grounds for introducing the sense of "breeze" or "wind" is not clear.

181

DAY 1

1. Gerard Manley Hopkins, SJ (1844–89), *God's Grandeur* (1877).

2. See Dennis T. Olson, "Genesis," in *New Interpreter's Bible: One Volume Commentary*, ed. B. R. Gaventa and D. Petersen (Nashville, TN: Abingdon, 2010), 4.

3. This reserve has its origins especially in the classic essay of Lynn White, "The Historical Roots of Our Ecological Crisis," originally a lecture given in Washington in 1966, subsequently published in *Science* 165 (1967): 1203–7, https://www.uvm.edu/~gflomenh/ENV-NGO-PA395/articles/Lynn-White.pdf.

4. Pope Francis deals at length with this issue of anthropocentrism in his encyclical *Laudato Si'* (2015), §§67–69.

5. The name *Adam* by which the first man is traditionally known simply stems from the Hebrew word *'adam*, which is not a proper name but simply denotes a male individual ("the man") or humankind in general.

6. Olson, "Genesis," 5.

7. "To be truly a creature entails limits; to honor limits becomes necessary if creation will develop as God intends. Yet, while the language takes the form of a command, the issue involves trust in the word of God. Decisions faced by the humans will concern not only themselves, but also choices that have implications for their relationship with *God*" (Terence E. Fretheim, "Genesis," in *NIB*, 1:351); see also Pope Francis, *Laudato Si'*, §66.

8. "Helper" may seem to imply lower status, the role of inferior assistant, but this is not necessarily the case: God is sometimes called a "helper" in the Old Testament (Pss 10:14; 54:4).

9. Fretheim, "Genesis," 355.

10. Charles Taylor, *A Secular Age* (Cambridge, MA; London, UK: Belnap, 2007), 277, also 67.

11. On this understanding of the opening verses of the Fourth Gospel, see further Brendan Byrne, *Life Abounding: A Reading of John's Gospel* (Collegeville, MN: Liturgical Press; Strathfield, NSW: St. Pauls, 2014), 22–25.

12. Notably, the gift of the Law to Israel through Moses (1:16–17).

13. Cf. Andrew T. Lincoln, "Colossians," in *NIB* XI, 597.

14. Untitled and undated (possibly 1877), first published in 1915.

15. The Greek word *huiothesia* is regularly and rightly, in view of its meaning in a secular context, translated "adoption." The legal term *adoption*, however, does not quite catch the intimacy and familiarity inherent in the term emerging from a biblical and Jewish background. *Huiothesia* designates a "family" relationship with God that Paul reckons among the distinct privileges uniquely enjoyed by Israel over and against the remainder of the world (Rom 9:4–5). Of course, God is not the "Father" of Israel in a literal, generative sense; in this respect *adoption* reflects the metaphorical sense in which the relationship must be understood. It is important, however, to preserve the familiar intimacy that is clearly connoted by the term in Pauline contexts such as Rom 8:15 and Gal 4:6–7.

DAY 2

1. Cf. Fretheim, "Genesis," 360.

2. Ibid., 363b.

3. "Creation, Creativity, and Creatureliness: The Wisdom of Finite Existence," in *Being in Creation: Human Responsibility in an Endangered World*, ed. Brian Treanor, Bruce Ellis Benson, and Norman Wirzba (New York: Fordham University Press, 2015), 23–36, 187 (Notes), at 33.

DAY 3

1. See especially "Rules for Discernment" §313, 326.

2. See J. P. Sampley, "1 Corinthians," in *NIB* XI.93a.

3. See Brendan Byrne, *Romans*, Sacra Pagina 6 (Collegeville, MN: Glazier, 1996), 176–77.

DAY 4

1. See Luke Timothy Johnson, *The Acts of the Apostles*, Sacra Pagina 5 (Collegeville, MN: Liturgical Press, 1992), 168.

2. Perhaps the best clue is provided by a jibe he mentions in 2 Cor 10:10: "His letters are weighty and strong, but his bodily presence is weak, and his speech contemptible."

3. Such direction is rather like tuning a radio: turning the knob too far counterclockwise (the past) or clockwise (the future) results in static in both cases; landing on the precise frequency (the present) gets the sound right.

DAY 5

1. The purpose for which Paul wrote Romans remains a matter of scholarly dispute. For the view presented here, see my commentary *Romans*, 8–9; also, more briefly, Brendan Byrne, *Galatians and Romans* (Collegeville, MN: Liturgical Press, 2010), 53–56.

2. The famous (at least for Jesuits) confession that stands at the head of the "Jesuits Today" document of General Congregation (1974–75), "What is it to be a Jesuit? It is to know that one is a sinner, yet called to be a companion of Jesus" (GC 32, §11), is in this way totally in conformity with the Pauline notion of faith.

3. "Christ did not begin where Adam began. He had to begin where Adam ended, that is, by taking on to himself not merely a clean slate, not merely even the single sin of Adam, but the whole entail of that sin, working its way out in the 'many sins' of Adam's descendants" (N. T. Wright, "Adam, Israel and the Messiah," in *The Climax of the Covenant: Christ and the Law in Pauline Theology* [Edinburgh: T&T Clark, 1991], 18–40, at 37).

4. In the Greek word *charisma*, which normally refers in Paul to a gift of the Spirit (as particularly in 1 Cor 12—14), the *–ma* ending here adds to *charis* the meaning of a concrete embodiment of God's grace seen in the human life and mission of the Son.

5. In this connection, we might note that a comment of future accountability is not absent from Paul. He reminds the Corinthians that "all of us must appear before the judgment seat of Christ, so that each may receive recompense for what has been done in the body, whether good or evil" (2 Cor 5:10). The gift of righteousness must be lived out in our bodily life through the power of the Spirit (Rom 8:5–11).

DAY 6

1. *Metamorphoses*, 7:19–21.

2. See Brendan Byrne, *Romans*, 233.

3. The ecumenical implications of the passive ("might be fulfilled in us") are significant. It respects the Protestant insistence on divine initiative and grace, while preserving the Catholic sense that the good "works" of believers—while entirely the product of the Spirit within them—really do contribute to God's future for humanity and the world.

4. Rom 1:16–17 has long been recognized as stating the overall theme of the letter, introducing it as an exposition of the gospel.

5. The Greek word *huiothesia* is usually translated "adoption" because that is the meaning in which it regularly appears in secular Greek literature and inscriptions of the time. Adoption, however, was not commonly practiced among Jews and the word designates a single act (of adoption) rather than the enduring (filial) status that seems to be called for, both by the biblical background of the motif and Paul's own usage. To express the enduring status, I employ the term *sonship*—non-inclusive, it is true, but seemingly necessary to avoid the cumbersome, albeit accurate paraphrase "status of sons and daughters" (see Gal 3:26).

6. It is regrettable that Pope Francis's encyclical *Laudato Si'* while drawing richly on biblical texts from Genesis and other parts of the Old Testament, makes a bare reference to the earth's "groaning in travail" (Rom 8:22) in an opening paragraph (§2), and then fails to return to this surely relevant Pauline text.

7. See Pope Francis, *Laudato Si'*, §§67–68.

DAY 7

1. Any hint of a "forensic" (lawcourt) context comes from the Jewish apocalyptic expectation of an impending divine judgment of the world that is an essential background to Paul's thought and argument. Paul evokes this judgment scene in Rom 8:31–39 precisely to affirm that it holds "no [prospect of] condemnation"

(Rom 8:1) for those who have received the gift of righteousness in Christ Jesus and live out that righteousness faithfully through the power of the Spirit (8:5–11).

2. From the first stanza of "Bring, all ye dear-bought nations bring," a traditional English hymn based loosely on the Latin Sequence for Easter Sunday, *Victimae Paschali Laudes*.

DAY 8

1. In Corinth, the idea of a risen existence seems to have come into question. Although written decades later, Paul's speech to the Athenians in Acts 17 at the Areopagus shows how Paul's commendation of the gospel in another Greek city runs into turbulence at the mention of resurrection from the dead (17:32).

2. The word *tagma* is used of a detachment of soldiers or, more generally, of a distinct group of people.

3. This psalm is more widely the subject of quotation and allusion in the New Testament than any other Old Testament text. It clearly played a central role in the developing understanding of the status and mission of Christ from the earliest days of the post-Easter Christian movement.

4. Here again we have the personification of "Death," as in Rom 5:12–21.

5. From the familiar Grail version, although I ask forbearance for the noninclusive language.

6. See Ernst Käsemann, "Ministry and Community in the New Testament," in *Essays on New Testament Themes* (London: SCM, 1964, 1981), 63–94, esp. 64–68.

7. We see here stretched out as a program, so to speak, the vision of the third stanza of the hymn (Phil 2:9–11), which in its poetic way sees the subjection of "all things" as already accomplished. The last line of the hymn ("to the glory of God the Father") corresponds to the "handing over of the kingdom to the Father" in 1 Cor 15:24, 28.

8. The ultimate aim flowing from this love is the free, joyful, and trusting surrender of my life-project to God expressed in the *Sume et Suscipe* ("Take and Receive") prayer in the same exercise (§234).

9. In Paul's sustained indictment of the alienation from God (lapse into idolatry) of the Gentile world in Rom 1:18–32, the archetypal failure to honor God is accompanied by failure to "give thanks" (1:21). The proclamation of the gospel is designed precisely to reverse that failure.

10. One essential feature of love that I have always sensed to be missing from Paul's list—and one that is surely particularly relevant for those about to be married—is that love is always ready to say "sorry" and to seek forgiveness and reconciliation.

11. This is, of course, the central issue running through Rom 9—11, culminating in the magnificent declarations of 11:25–32, especially the statement that "the gifts and calling of God are irrevocable" (v. 29).

12. See especially the short "excursus on hope" that appears a few sentences before the passage we are considering in verses 24–25. Here Paul insists that a hope that is "seen" (i.e., clearly discerned) is not really hope at all. One hopes for what one does not (yet) see.

13. The Catholic doctrine of the Assumption of Mary, otherwise resting entirely on Tradition, may find some biblical foundation here.

14. Author's translation from the Latin.

FURTHER READING

Byrne, Brendan. *Galatians and Romans*. Collegeville, MN: Liturgical Press, 2010. A short commentary on both letters designed for a general readership.

———. *Inheriting the Earth: The Pauline Basis of a Spirituality for Our Time*. Homebush, NSW: St. Paul Publications, 1990; New York: Alba House, 1991. A presentation of Pauline spirituality based on Paul's Letter to the Romans.

———. *Romans*. Sacra Pagina 6. Collegeville, MN: Liturgical Press, 1996. A scholarly commentary on Romans with a strong theological emphasis.

Campbell, Antony F. *God First Loved Us: The Challenge of Accepting Unconditional Love*. New York: Paulist Press, 2000. An engaging, deeply pondered work by a noted Old Testament scholar that brings a comprehensive biblical background to a central Pauline theme.

Dunn, James D. G. *The Theology of Paul the Apostle*. Grand Rapids, MI; Cambridge, UK: Eerdmans, 1998. A comprehensive and reliable compendium of Paul's theology by an outstanding British Pauline scholar.

Fitzmyer, Joseph A. *Spiritual Exercises Based on Paul's Epistle to the Romans*. New York: Paulist Press, 1995. As the title states, this work traces the Spiritual Exercises in the Letter to the Romans.

Harrington, Daniel J. *Meeting St. Paul Today: Understanding the Man, His Mission, and His Message*. Chicago: Loyola Press, 2008. A very reader-friendly and reliable introduction to Paul by a great scholar.

Hooker, Morna D. *Pauline Pieces*. London: Epworth, 1979; reprinted Eugene, OR: Wipf and Stock, 2006. This slim volume has successfully introduced a wide audience to Paul over many decades.

Horrell, David G. *An Introduction to the Study of Paul*. 2nd ed. London and New York: T&T Clark, 2006. An outstanding introduction to Paul and his theology; scholarly but very accessible.

Matera, Frank J. *Romans*. Paideia. Grand Rapids, MI: Baker Academic, 2010. A fine commentary on the letter, matching up-to-date scholarship with high pedagogical skill and pastoral concern.

Stegman, Thomas D. "Run That You May Obtain the Prize: Using St. Paul as a Resource for the Spiritual Exercises," *Studies in the Spirituality of Jesuits* 44, no. 4 (Winter 2012). This article provides an up-to-date introduction to Paul's theology, followed by an annotated list of texts suggested for an eight-day Ignatian retreat.

Trilling, Wolfgang. *A Conversation with Paul*. London: SCM, 1986. An engaging exposition of Paul's theology marked by critical awareness of the challenges it presents for readers today.

Wright, N. Thomas. *Paul for Everyone*. A series of popular introductions to Paul's letters jointly published by SPCK (London) and Westminster John Knox (Louisville, KY) as follows: *Romans* (2 vols., 2004); *Corinthians* (2 vols., 2003–4); *Galatians and Thessalonians* (2004); *The Prison Letters: Ephesians, Philippians, Colossians and Philemon* (2004); *The Pastoral Letters: 1 and 2 Timothy and Titus* (2004).

SCRIPTURE INDEX

OLD TESTAMENT

APOCRYPHA

NEW TESTAMENT

Scripture Index